N

D0771856

SIMONE WEIL: LECTURES ON PHILOSOPHY

SIMONE WEIL

Lectures on philosophy

TRANSLATED BY HUGH PRICE

WITH AN INTRODUCTION BY PETER WINCH

CAMBRIDGE UNIVERSITY PRESS

CAMBRIDGE

LONDON · NEW YORK · MELBOURNE

Published by the Syndics of the Cambridge University Press
The Pitt Building, Trumpington Street, Cambridge CB2 1RP
Bentley House, 200 Euston Road, London NW1 2DB
32 East 57th Street, New York, NY 10022, USA
296 Beaconsfield Parade, Middle Park, Melbourne 3206, Australia

First published 1978

PRINTED IN GREAT BRITAIN
AT THE UNIVERSITY PRESS, CAMBRIDGE

Library of Congress Cataloguing in Publication Data

Weil, Simone, 1909–1943.
Lectures on philosophy.

Translation of Leçons de philosophie.
1. Philosophy – Addresses, essays, lectures.
I. Title.
B2430.W473L3513   194   77-26735

ISBN 0 521 22005 X hard cover
ISBN 0 521 29333 2 paperback

Contents

5   Miscellaneous topics and essay plans   190

Index

Translator's preface

Although most of Simone Weil's published writings are now available in English, I feel that English readers will be interested in these notes of her lectures, taken down by Madame Anne Reynaud-Guérithault when she was a pupil in a girls' *lycée* at Roanne where Simone Weil taught philosophy in the school year 1933–4. Madame Reynaud-Guérithault herself warns us that these are one pupil's hastily written notes and not a verbatim record of the lectures. Nevertheless they provide us with a fascinating glimpse of Simone Weil the teacher. In 'hearing' her trace the history of thought for her pupils, one hears echoes of her own philosophical training. But one is also struck by her breadth of knowledge and understanding, clarity of expression and, most forcibly of all, by her almost visionary ability to draw together strands of knowledge from many different fields. She deals here with a wide range of topics and so the book in itself is a good introduction to philosophy. Those who already know her later writings in translation will be interested to find them hinted at in part in these earlier thoughts.

The *Leçons de philosophie* were first published in French by Plon (1959). I have added brief explanatory notes on some of the references in the text which might be unfamiliar to English-speaking students using this as a first introduction to philosophy.

I would like to thank all those who, in one way or another, showed an interest in and helped with this translation or the notes. They are too many to name. Peter Winch has very kindly written the introduction.

September 1977   Hugh Price

Introduction

Five weeks before her death in August 1943 Simone Weil wrote
a letter from London to her parents in New York in which she
briefly discussed the attitude of her contemporaries to her work.
Replying to a remark in a letter from her mother, she wrote:

Darling M., you think I have something to give. That is badly
expressed. But I too have a sort of growing inner certainty
that there is a deposit of pure gold in me which ought to be
passed on. The trouble is that I am more and more con-
vinced by my experience and observation of my contemporaries that there is no one to receive it.

It's a dense mass. What gets added to it is of a piece with
the rest. As the mass grows it becomes more and more
dense. I can't parcel it out into little pieces.

It would require an effort to come to terms with it. And
making an effort is so tiring!

Some people feel vaguely that there is something there. But
they content themselves with uttering a few eulogistic epithets
about my intelligence and that completely satisfies their
conscience. Then they listen to me or read me with the same
fleeting attention they give everything else, taking each little
fragment of an idea as it comes along and making a definitive
mental decision: 'I agree with this', 'I don't agree with that',
'this is brilliant', 'that is completely mad' (that last antithesis
comes from my boss). They conclude: 'It's very interesting',

and then go on to something else. They haven't tired themselves.[1]

That is a characteristically shrewd diagnosis and it is hardly less
applicable to the situation now, thirty-four years after her death,
than it was then. Her work has many different facets and it is not
always easy to see the relation between them. But, while it would
be a mistake to think of her as having produced a tight philosophical 'system', her treatments of apparently disparate topics do
hang together and frequently cannot be adequately grasped or
evaluated without a view of the relation between them. There are
obstacles in the way of attaining such a view. Some of these stem
from the difficulty of 'placing' her work firmly within any
currently living tradition of thinking. (The disintegration of con-
temporary culture which is partly responsible for this was of course
one of the great themes to which Simone Weil addressed herself.)
Perhaps this difficulty is greater for English-speaking than for
French readers; and it has been exacerbated by the piecemeal way
in which her writings have appeared in English translation.

'Professional philosophers' have by no means been in the fore-
front of those who have taken an interest in her work. Part of the
reason for this is that, though the pieces which have already
appeared in English translation do often contain discussions of
themes which exercise Anglo-Saxon academic philosophers, these
occur in contexts, and in a style, which may create the impression
that their bearing on the central concerns of such philosophers
is at best a glancing one.

Of the writings that have hitherto been available in French, but
not in English, there are two which deal directly and extensively
with fundamental conceptual and philosophical issues of a sort
which are never (or never should be) far away from the centre
of a philosopher's attention. These are *Science et perception dans
Descartes*[2] and *Leçons de philosophie*, which latter now happily, if
belatedly, reaches English readers for the first time in Dr Hugh
Price's excellent translation. *Science et perception* is an immature

---

[1] *Ecrits de Londres* (Gallimard, Paris 1957), p. 250.
[2] In *Sur la Science* (Gallimard, Paris 1966).

piece, written as a dissertation for the *diplome d'études supérieures* in 1929–30. While it contains points of great interest, the four-year interval which separates it from *Lectures on Philosophy* marks a considerable increase in maturity and a much firmer sense of direction. The *Lectures* do not come directly from Simone Weil's own hand but consist of notes of her lectures at the Roanne *lycée* taken by Madame Anne Reynaud-Guérithault, one of her students in 1933–4. These notes are remarkably full and have obviously been taken and transcribed with great care and sensitivity. While it is inevitable that there should be moments when one wonders whether one is getting quite completely what Simone Weil had to say about a certain topic, such moments are surprisingly rare. I think there is no doubt that we have here a very substantial presentation of what was said in the lectures. Those who are familiar with Simone Weil's own writings will also at once recognise the authentic sound of her own voice. Madame Reynaud's achievement is, by any standards, very remarkable and there must be very few lecturers in philosophy who have come across such an intelligent and faithful rendering of their teaching in notes taken by students – let alone by students of that age. What surprises one here is not just the ability to reproduce the teacher's actual words but the understanding conveyed in the presentation of what is said about very difficult and complex issues.

I have suggested that these lectures can be distinguished from most of Simone Weil's writings in being directly concerned with fundamental 'philosophical' issues. The suggestion has to be taken with caution in so far as it may seem to imply some firm and generally agreed distinction between what is a philosophical issue and what is not. But this is not of course so; and Simone Weil's later writings, particularly, raise in a very acute form the difficulty of making such a distinction; she is inclined to import ideas which have been developed in what can be recognised quite uncontroversially as philosophical discussions into reflections which seem to have a very different character – that of religious meditation for example. This raises puzzling questions about how these writings are to be taken and how they are related to 'philosophy'. Similar questions are liable to be raised by the work of any truly innovative thinker.

It may help English-speaking readers, familiar with the con-
temporary philosophical scene in this country, to come to grips
with *Lectures on Philosophy* if I compare them with the ideas which
Ludwig Wittgenstein was developing independently in Cambridge
at about the same time. (Hugh Price has reminded me that Wittgenstein dictated his *Blue Book* during the same academic year as
that in which these lectures were being given.)

In about 1930 Wittgenstein wrote:

> There is not – as I used to believe – a primary language as
> opposed to our ordinary language, the 'secondary' one. But
> one could speak of a primary language as opposed to ours in
> so far as the former would not permit any way of expressing
> a preference for certain phenomena over others; it would
> have to be, so to speak, absolutely *impartial*.[1]

The context makes it clear that the supposed 'primary' language
which is in question would be 'phenomenological' in character and
that its 'impartiality' would in part consist in its expressing
immediate experience without commitment to any conception of
a spatio-temporally ordered world of physical objects.

In *Science et perception dans Descartes* Simone Weil had attempted
to take such a phenomenological language as a starting point, and
to trace how the conception of such a world can develop from it.
The main central section of that work is a meditation, self-
consciously in the Cartesian manner, which starts with an attempt
to describe an undifferentiated flux of sensations; she tries to show
how the distinction between 'I' and 'the world' which confronts
me, but to which I also in some sense belong, arises through an
ordering of this phenomenological world, brought about by the
methodical application of operations (such as elementary arithmetical and geometrical constructions) to it. Her main divergence
from Descartes consists in an insistence that the word 'I' does not
stand for a substantial subject of consciousness, but is simply the
expression of such methodical activity. This approach leads her
into several, half-recognised, tangles. Not least of these is the diffi-

[1] *Philosophical Remarks*, trans. Raymond Hargreaves and Roger White
(Blackwell, Oxford 1975), p. 84.

culty of giving any clear account of the relation between 'I' as expressing pure activity and the role of the human body in activity.

She rejects the idea that the word 'I' stands for an object that acts on other objects; her view could be expressed by saying that it functions as the purely grammatical subject of verbs of activity. The active element in all such verbs is *thought*. Simone Weil's idea (in *Science et perception*) seems to be something like this: My activity is constituted by everything that I completely control: everything, and only that, which is completely expressive of myself. This includes only what is completely transparent to my understanding, since anything in my experience that I do not understand is something that I *undergo* or am simply confronted with – all this belongs to the realm of what she calls '*hasard*' or contingency. The movements of my body, therefore, cannot be exclusively an expression of my activity, since those movements depend on contingent factors which I have to accept for what they are, which are not themselves a product of my activity. The idea is very close to that expressed by the early Wittgenstein:

> Even if all that we wish for were to happen, still this would only be a favour granted by fate, so to speak: for there is no *logical* connexion between the will and the world, which would guarantee it, and the supposed physical connexion itself is surely not something that we could will.[1]

So the conception of bodily activity is left shrouded in mystery in *Science et perception*, as it is in the *Tractatus*. The difficulty at this stage for both Wittgenstein and Simone Weil is to reconcile the possibility of making assertions, or having thoughts, which are *about* something (which have a relation to 'the world') and the possibility of acting. Both writers lean heavily on the notion of activity (in the form of 'performing operations' in Wittgenstein's case) in their account of thinking, but neither of them introduces the notion of action into the account at an early enough stage. In the *Tractatus* operations are performed on elementary propositions which are regarded as assertible prior to the performance of those operations (they are the 'bases' on which operations are

[1] *Tractatus Logico-Philosophicus*, 6.374, trans. D. F. Pears and B. F. McGuinness (Routledge & Kegan Paul, London 1961).

performed). Yet it is essential to elementary propositions that they
have a 'structure'; and the only explicit account of structure, or
form, which the *Tractatus* offers relies on the application of logical
operations *on* elementary propositions, which have to be taken, as
it were, as 'given' for this purpose. And in *Science et perception* it
is implicitly presupposed that a primitive, passively undergone,
phenomenology of sensation can be described before the notion
of 'activity' is introduced: for activity needs something to work on.
Yet in reality the internal logic of both positions demands that
activity is involved in the possibility of having thoughts about
anything whatever: in the possibility of asserting elementary propositions in the *Tractatus*, and in the possibility of describing one's
experience in *Science et perception*. That is to say, the difficulty in
offering an intelligible account of the relation between thought
and action, which both of them encounter, is not a local one; it
is a difficulty for the whole account of thought that is being offered.
Both Wittgenstein and Simone Weil came to realise this as their
ideas developed; and both, interestingly, expressed this realisation
by insisting on the importance of the line from Goethe's *Faust*: 'In
the beginning was the deed'.[1]

The nature of their difficulty emerges more clearly if we ask how
the 'operations' of which they both speak are to be understood.
In the *Tractatus* the operations are performed on 'propositions'.
These are not identical with 'propositional signs', for 'a proposition is a propositional sign in its projective relation to the world'
(3.12). How is this 'projective relation' to be understood? It looks
as though it must be a feature of how the sign is *used*; but this must
mean that the user is active in relation to the sign. A sign is a
physical existent and so its use must involve an actual physical
manipulation. (In effect Wittgenstein is insisting on this when,
later, he remarks: 'We are talking about the spatial and temporal
phenomenon of language, not about some non-spatial, non-
temporal phantasm';[2] and Simone Weil is making a similar point

---

[1] See Simone Weil, *First and Last Notebooks*, trans. Richard Rees (Oxford
University Press, 1970), p. 24; Ludwig Wittgenstein, *On Certainty*, trans.
Denis Paul and G. E. M. Anscombe (Blackwell, Oxford 1969), p. 51.

[2] *Philosophical Investigations*, trans. G. E. M. Anscombe (Blackwell, Oxford
1953), I, ‡ 108.

in *Lectures on Philosophy* in what she says about the 'manageability' of words and of geometrical figures.) Hence the idea of voluntary physical activity, at least in the form of speaking or writing, must already be involved in that of a 'proposition' and any difficulty concerning the possibility of such activity, of voluntary bodily movement, will infect the account of what a proposition is. If we cannot make sense of what it is to act with our bodies, neither can we make sense of what it is to think that something is the case.

In Simone Weil's *Science et perception* an analogous difficulty emerges in a different form. The conception of a 'world' about which I can have intelligible thoughts requires that I experience things as ordered in definite series. Order is not something empirically given, but is something which I construct in reacting methodically to the situations confronting me. But the very conception of 'situations confronting me' already seems to imply an order (just as the elementary propositions of the *Tractatus* already have a structure). And the conception of 'reacting methodically' seems to imply that my body has a special place in my world: I control its movements directly in a sense in which I do not directly control the movements of anything else. And yet, as I have already remarked, Simone Weil's conception of activity at this stage is not explicable in terms of controlled bodily movement, since this is subject to empirically given conditions not themselves under my control. The trouble comes from the apparently unbridgeable gulf that she seems to be creating between, on the one hand, an experience which is entirely passively undergone, in which everything is on a level, equally a matter of '*hasard*' and, on the other hand, an etherealised conception of activity which is divorced from bodily movement.

In *Lectures on Philosophy* her perspective has dramatically shifted. Instead of trying to start with a phenomenological description of 'immediate present experience' in the first person singular, she adopts what she calls 'the materialist point of view'. She draws attention to familiar situations in which we observe human beings physically reacting to their environments and tries to show how these reactions form the basis of concept formation. The notion of activity is not etherealised, as it had been in *Science et perception*:

it is exhibited, mainly in chapter 2, as a refinement and development of the primitive reactions described in chapter 1.

Chapter 1 also spells out the reasons for this shift in perspective.
The question she is considering here is: how is our conception of
the world of spatio-temporal objects, with definite, recognisable
properties and ways of interacting, related to our sense experience? It may seem natural to approach this question, after the
manner of *Science et perception*, by starting with a description of
our sense experience 'as it is in itself', without allowing any
reference to physical things. Then, it may seem, we can examine
how reference to such things can grow out of, be based on, the
experience thus described. But our attempted description runs
into difficulties straightaway. Suppose I say that I see a red, square
patch. To say that it is 'red' is to apply the concept of colour and
to locate the colour of *this* patch by reference to other possible
colours it might have. Colours belong to a 'series'. If this patch
is red, it is not green or blue: that is implied by my description.
(One may notice here how recognition of this fact played an
important part in the development of Wittgenstein's criticisms of
his earlier conception of 'elementary propositions'.)[1] Similar
considerations apply to the description of the patch as 'square'.
But how can such implications be 'given', 'presented' to me by
my present experience of the patch? I am in a position to see the
implications, and hence to describe the patch at all, only in so far
as I am *already* competent in the use of the terms I apply to it;
only in so far as I am versed in the application of terms like 'red',
'blue', 'green', or 'square', 'round', 'triangular', etc., in other
situations. But, if this is a general truth, I cannot have directly
drawn such an ability, cannot have derived my concepts, from *any*
particular experience I have had because, whichever I choose, the
same difficulty can be made.

The difficulty is one involving the notion of time; and it is a virtue
of Simone Weil's discussion that she emphasises fundamental
difficulties in applying temporal notions within the context of such
a primitive 'phenomenology'. I can only describe what I experi-

[1] See, for example, *Philosophical Grammar*, trans. Anthony Kenny (Blackwell, Oxford 1974), pp. 210–11.

ence *now* by bringing it into some determinate relation with what I have experienced in the past and what I may experience in the future. (This is not a regrettable incapacity, but a feature of what we should be prepared to call a 'description'.) But, we want to ask, what have past and future got to do with the experience I am having *now*? They seem to be quite external to that experience and the whole point of the phenomenological description was supposed to be that it fastened on something which could, considered in itself, provide a basis for our concepts.

> As far as the sensation itself is concerned, one cannot think of it except by actually feeling it. A past sensation, or one to come, is then absolutely nothing, and, as a result, since sensations have significance only in relation to the present moment, there is in them no passing of time and they do not give us the idea of time. (p. 46)

It won't help to talk of a 'specious present', or a 'duration' (Bergson), which belongs to sensations considered in themselves. This would still be nothing but an internal property of them and would not serve to relate them to each other in the necessary way.

Can we perhaps overcome the difficulty by introducing the notion of *remembering* that the sensation I am having now is like one I have had in the past? How should this be understood? If we take remembering to be another present experience, which I have contemporaneously with the sensation, then that is all it is – another present experience. And how could *that* provide a connection with other experiences had in the past? Indeed how can I so much as think, from this perspective, of 'experiences had in the past'? I am supposed to be confined to description of my *present* experiences! A natural objection here would be to say that remembering, unlike sensation, as it were overflows the present moment; it has an essential reference to something in the past. This is no doubt true. But when we speak of remembering in this, the normal way, we are not describing a present experience.[1] We are speaking in a way which already incapsulates a relation

[1] For an illuminating discussion of the ramifications of this point, see Norman Malcolm's *Memory and Mind* (Cornell University Press, 1977).

between present and past; but the whole difficulty is to see how this is possible within the context of a 'phenomenology of the present experience'. The language we actually do speak does of course contain this possibility, but it cannot be derived from any feature of a present experience. To remember a past event is already to locate oneself in a spatio-temporal order; and what is at issue is the nature of one's ability to do just this.

There is worse to come. We have been talking blithely about 'present' experience. But what can this mean? We understand the word 'present' in relation to 'past' and 'future'. If we have no way of talking about these we have no way of talking about 'present' either; in fact we have no way of talking.

> On the contrary, it is impossible to limit sensations to the
> present moment; to say that sensations are limited to the pres-
> ent moment would be to locate them once again in time.
> (p. 00)

That remark may be compared with the following by Wittgenstein:

> If someone says, only the *present* experience has reality, then
> the word 'present' must be redundant here, as the word 'I'
> is in other contexts. For it cannot mean *present* as opposed to
> past and future. . . . Something else must be meant by the
> word, something that isn't *in* a space, but is itself a space.
> That is to say, not something bordering on something else
> (from which it could therefore be limited off). . . . And so,
> something language cannot legitimately set in relief. And
> so it ['present'] is a meaningless epithet.[1]

There is more than a superficial similarity between Wittgenstein's and Simone Weil's thinking on this point. Like her, he is trying to come to terms with his earlier conception of our everyday language as somehow 'secondary', as based on a 'primary', 'phenomenological' language. And again, he too is trying to do justice to the idea that, if my thought is to have the kind of link with the world which is involved in its being 'about' something,

---

[1] *Philosophical Remarks*, p. 85.

then there must be something about my relation to the world at the time I express the thought which constitutes that link.

> The stream of life, or the stream of the world, flows on and our propositions are so to speak verified only at instants. Our propositions are only verified by the present. So they must be so constructed that they can be verified by it.[1]

Both are making the point that it is a misconception to suppose that the link between our propositions and what puts us into the position of being able to assert them, is an immediate relation to, as it were, a raw experience. Both try to show that the conception of an experience, in the sense of an appearance to me which is without commitment to the 'real' features of what it is an appearance of, is not a datum, but a highly sophisticated construction, *presupposing* our ordinary ways of thinking about physical objects: not 'primary', but itself 'secondary'.

I have emphasised that these criticisms of empiricist accounts of concept formation to a large extent revolve round the inability of such accounts to give any coherent account of *time*. Time is essential to the idea of a connection between experiences; and it is only by virtue of such a connection that experiences are describable or graspable. On the empiricist view time becomes an unbridgeable gulf between one experience and another. We need an account which, on the contrary, will include time as a form of connection between experiences. Simone Weil's account, like Wittgenstein's, achieves this by making the notion of *action* central. Action is conceived, in the first instance, as a series of bodily movements having a certain determinate temporal order. In its primitive form action is quite unreflective. Human beings, and other animate creatures, naturally react in characteristic ways to objects in their environments. They salivate in the presence of food and eat it; this already effects a rudimentary classification (which doesn't have to be based on any reflection) between 'food' and 'not food'. Our eyes scan objects and connect with other characteristic movements of our bodies, we sniff things (or sometimes hold our noses), we exhibit subtly different reactions to

[1] *Ibid.* p. 81.

things we put into our mouths – corresponding to such classifications of tastes as 'sour', 'sweet', 'salty', etc. – and so on. These reactions are refined and developed as we mature; and some of these refinements and developments are responses to training by other human beings around us. A staircase is something to be climbed, a chair something to be sat in: compare Wittgenstein's remark: 'It is part of the grammar of the word "chair" that *this* is what we call "to sit on a chair".'[1] As Simone Weil expresses it: 'everything that we see suggests some kind of movement' (p. 31).

It is natural to think of our reactions to objects as based on a prior recognition of their qualities. Of course there are plenty of situations which can perfectly well be so described; but they are cases in which we *already* exhibit forms of reaction in the context of which it makes sense to say that we recognise the qualities in question. Our recognition of the qualities of things, in its most primitive form, is itself expressed in characteristic reactions; reflective action – action based on a prior recognition – is a subsequent, more sophisticated stage, presupposing the prior formation of appropriate concepts. Simone Weil sums up her position in a striking image:

> The very nature of the relationship between ourselves and what is external to us, a relationship which consists in a reaction, a reflex, is our perception of the external world. Perception of nature, pure and simple, is a sort of dance; it is this dance that makes perception possible for us. (p. 52)

I remarked earlier that a major difficulty in her previous approach to these questions in *Science et perception* was as follows. The conception of a world which can be studied implies the notion of order; and order is not something 'given' – 'The world, in a storm, is not going to provide us with 1 grain, then 2, then 3 grains of sand' (p. 71). Order is *constructed* by methodical activity in relation to the situations confronting one. But, I suggested, the very idea of being confronted with determinate situations to which one might react methodically seems itself to imply a pre-existing order.

[1] *The Blue and Brown Books* (Blackwell, Oxford 1958), p. 24.

The new account of perception in *Lectures on Philosophy* shows how this is possible.

> When we are on the point of giving birth to thought, it comes to birth in a world that already is ordered. (p. 32)

This order, which is not a result, but a precondition, of thought is introduced by the unreflective 'dance' of the body.

Roughly speaking chapter 2 tries to exhibit thought as a development and refinement of this primitive dance of the body. Unreflective reactions evolve into *methodical* action. This evolution brings with it the notion of an 'obstacle'. I may not be able to obtain food by simply stretching out my hand; perhaps the fruit is out of my reach up a tree. I turn *away* from the tree and look for a stick with which I can knock the fruit down. It is an important and striking feature of Simone Weil's account of methodical action that it emphasises this 'turning away', the renunciation of immediate satisfaction in favour of doing something else which does not lead directly to what I seek. The image of a sailing boat tacking against the wind is one she often uses to great effect to bring the point out. It is, I think, quite instructive to think of the typical activities which make up our daily lives from this point of view; to notice how much of what we do has this feature of taking us apparently, in the first instance, *away* from what we seek. At all events it is a way of thinking which plays a big part in what Simone Weil writes about a great many topics. In general it is important to the way she develops the idea of a natural order within which things happen according to certain necessities which are quite independent of our desires. The internal connection which she is suggesting holds between the apprehension of natural necessities and the renunciation of immediate satisfactions is the basis of some of her most arresting and provocative ideas on the moral and religious dimensions of science – for example in the essay 'Classical Science and After'.[1]

The account of necessity sketched in *Lectures on Philosophy* is one of the most interesting and important features of the book. Once

---

[1] In *On Science, Necessity and the Love of God*, trans. Richard Rees (Oxford University Press, 1968).

again there are striking affinities with Wittgenstein. Like him Simone Weil was preoccupied with the relation between what one might call 'conceptual' and 'natural' necessity, between the 'order' which characterises the relations between our ideas and the 'order' which we ascribe to the relations between things. This, of course, is an issue which must engage the attention of any serious philosopher; the affinity with Wittgenstein comes out in the way Simone Weil sees the key to this relation in the application of language in action.

Her main ideas appear most clearly in her discussion of mathematics. The use of mathematical techniques immeasurably increases our power to deal methodically with obstacles by, in the first place, introducing discriminations which are foreign to our unreflective perceptual reactions. Thus, up to a certain point, I can distinguish 'heavier' from 'lighter' objects simply by lifting them. But beyond the point at which I can no longer lift them they are all the same as far as I am concerned: they are 'too heavy' for me to lift. If however I can count, and apply techniques of weighing, I can distinguish something that weighs one ton from something that weighs two. Other techniques, such as the use of levers and pulleys, which presuppose the application of mathematics, enable me to manipulate and distinguish objects which would otherwise all be on a level: 'too heavy'.

It is a condition of such techniques that the mathematical notions which are applied in them should be subject to an order which is 'necessary' in the sense that they are, as it were, insulated from the accidents that experience may bring. Nothing is allowed to count against the equation $7+5 = 12$. The 'necessity' of this equation expresses the conditions under which we are prepared to apply these numbers to groups of objects and what we are willing to call 'addition'. If I count a group of five chairs, a group of seven chairs, put them together and then count thirteen, I do not say that in this case $7+5 = 13$. I say that I 'must' have miscounted somewhere, or that somehow another chair 'must' have been introduced without my noticing it. It is of course true *as a matter of fact* that I will usually be able to discover 'what has gone wrong' in such a case. This, along with countless similar facts, is what makes it worth hanging on to the strict equation $7+5 = 12$. But these are facts of experience, not necessities in the sense that '$7+5 = 12$' expresses a necessity. Such equations belong to the form which characterises what I am willing to allow as cases of 'counting', 'adding', etc. And it is the application of these expressions in the context of action, technique, which makes our insistence on the maintenance of certain unbreakable patterns in their use more than an idle game – which gives them the character of 'necessities'.

If we speak of 'necessities' in nature we are using the word in a way which derives from the necessities we insist on in the execution of our own methodical activities and in the interrelation between the concepts which are embedded in those activities. In applying concepts to natural phenomena we always work within an understood margin of error, corresponding to the particular techniques of application we are using. The refinement of such techniques brings with it a change in the margin of error allowed for in the application of our concepts. But it makes no sense to speak of a progressive *elimination* of margins of error, since their existence is internally connected with what we understand by an 'application of concepts'. In bringing out this point Simone Weil sometimes, dangerously and misleadingly, says that the empirical application of concepts always involves an 'infinite error'.[1] It is 'infinite' just because there can be no question of its progressive elimination. Far-reaching confusions are engendered if this is forgotten. But equally far-reaching confusions may be engendered by Simone Weil's suggestion that to apply concepts within a margin of error itself involves an 'error'. What needs to be recognised is that the very notion of an error (of the kind that is in question) *presupposes* the 'margin' allowed for in a technique of application. If we overlook this fundamental point we are liable to adopt the picture of a sort of super-necessity governing the relations between phenomena, analogous in kind to the necessity relating our concepts, but never fully captured in our actual

---

[1] See *On Science, Necessity and the Love of God*, p. 34. The seeds of this way of talking are discernible in some of the things she says in *Lectures on Philosophy*.

application of those concepts. And I think Simone Weil does sometimes fall prey to just such a picture[1] – I shall say a little more about this shortly. Sometimes – and this strikes me as less dangerous – she speaks of the application of concepts as 'hypothetical'. *If* such and such a term applies then certain determinate consequences necessarily follow: to the extent that those consequences are not realised experientially, there are grounds for mistrusting the original application of the term. 'If the equilibrium of a balance did not agree with the theory of the lever, one would say that there is something wrong with it' (p. 84).

I have tried to suggest some of the many striking parallels between the direction taken by Simone Weil's thinking and that of Wittgenstein. But there are also striking divergences. Perhaps one of the most fundamental is a strong systematising tendency in Simone Weil's thinking of a kind of which Wittgenstein was extremely, and increasingly, suspicious. This is nowhere more true than in her thinking about the notion of necessity. For instance, although her treatment of the relations between mathematics and the empirical sciences starts off in the same general direction as Wittgenstein's, there is nothing in her work to compare with the detailed examination of particular cases that is such a striking feature of, for example, Wittgenstein's discussion of the differences between mathematical calculation and physical experiment.[2] She is sometimes too ready to run together many different cases with a striking phrase: her talk about the 'infinite error' involved in the physical application of mathematics is a case in point. Again and connectedly, I have noted how, like Wittgenstein, she looks for the roots of the notion of necessity in human activities and techniques; but she is not struck in quite the same way as he is by the great *diversity* of such techniques. This led Wittgenstein to see a parallel diversity in the sense of terms like 'necessary'. Simone Weil is certainly sometimes sensitive to such considerations: a good example is her discussion of the philosophical difficulties created by failure to recognise the essential limits to the

[1] See, for instance, *Waiting on God* (Fontana Books, London 1959), p. 124.
[2] *Remarks on the Foundations of Mathematics*, trans. G. E. M. Anscombe (Blackwell, Oxford 1956).

application of a certain procedure and the closely connected tendency to confuse the application of two different procedures. (See, for instance, her discussion of incommensurability in the section on 'Mathematical invention', p. 113.)

But she also tends, sometimes in this work and much more so in later writings in which Plato's influence becomes more marked, to speak of the whole 'natural order' as subject to a *single* 'necessity'. This way of thinking is inextricably intertwined with her treatment of what is involved in facing affliction. She saw affliction as the inevitable concomitant of the 'necessity' of the natural order to which men are subject. In speaking in this way, she tended, rather like Spinoza, to confuse the senses of 'necessity' which apply to the natural laws established within science, with the fundamentally different sense of 'necessity' connected with ideas like 'fate'.

The seeds of this confusion are already present in the way she speaks, in *Lectures on Philosophy*, of the 'insufficiency' of science for the explanation of nature and of 'reality' as 'an obstacle which infinitely transcends us' (p. 111). As though there were a necessity in the natural world of which science gives us an inkling but can never quite reach out to. Whereas the notion of necessity that is in question when we talk, for instance, of a man as 'being defeated by the world' has little to do with the necessity involved in the workings of some (finite) obstacle. And the expression 'infinite obstacle' itself is really shown to be senseless by Simone Weil's own elucidation of the notion of an obstacle as of something that we can in principle try methodically to overcome. The following remark of Wittgenstein's is pertinent here:

> Fate stands in *contrast* with natural law.
> A natural law is something we establish and make use of, but this is not true of fate.[1]

I believe that attention to this issue, based on a study of what Simone Weil says about necessity in this book, would shed much light on problems involved in some of her most arresting and

---

[1] *Vermischte Bemerkungen* (Suhrkamp, Frankfurt a.M. 1977), p. 117 (my emphasis).

characteristic positions, as developed in her better known later writings.

Finally, I should like to say something about the relation between Simone Weil's epistemological discussions and her treatment of the social dimensions of human life. The notion of *activity* which, as I have indicated, is central to her account of concept-formation is on the whole treated in a very individualistic way in *Lectures on Philosophy*. It is true that her discussion of language emphasises some of the debts which the thinking of individual men owes to the cultural heritage transmitted to them through language. But this discussion is not fully integrated into her treatment of the notion of methodical action, which bears most of the weight in her account of thought. This is strikingly apparent if one sets her account alongside Wittgenstein's, with its emphasis on the mutual understanding involved in 'following a rule' and on the importance of 'training' in the acquisition of concepts. By contrast, in *Lectures on Philosophy*, Simone Weil concentrates her attention mainly on the attempts of an individual to attain his own ends and on the growth of methodical action out of his encounters and attempts to deal with obstacles in the way of those ends. In this respect her thinking retains a strong flavour of Cartesian individualism.

This is connected with the way she treats social oppression in the section on 'Sociology'. Both here and in some of the essays in *Oppression and Liberty*, oppression is seen as fundamentally an interference with the freedom of the individual to pursue his own projects in his own way through the use of his own intelligence. Conversely, the exercise of intelligent thought by individuals, being necessary to the continued life of social 'collectivities', is seen as one of the most important limits to the oppressive power of those collectivities. While what she says on this subject is important and seems to me to contain much truth, it does often lead to a comparative neglect of the social conditions which make the thought of individuals possible. The dependence on other people which is a necessary feature of life in a society is treated as a limitation on the individual's freedom and therefore *ipso facto* an oppressive tendency which one must try to minimise.

To the extent to which a man's fate is dependent on other men, his own life escapes not only out of his own hands, but also out of the control of his intelligence; judgement and resolution no longer have anything to which to apply themselves; instead of contriving and acting, one has to stoop to pleading and threatening. . . .[1]

It is obviously an exaggerated distortion to say that the only possible demeanour of men whose relations involve the dependence of one on another is either 'pleading' or 'threatening'. Simone Weil is led to say this precisely because she has developed the notion of understanding almost exclusively via the encounter of individual men with natural (physical) obstacles. She sees, rightly, that the relation of one man to another, just because men are intelligent agents, must be different from the relation of a man to a natural obstacle, and now finds it difficult to see how that relation can involve any mutual understanding: 'the human mind can never be understood or handled from the outside' (*ibid.*).

The situation in Wittgenstein's work is very different. There the mutual understanding expressed in 'agreement in judgements' is a condition of the formation of concepts of natural phenomena. Simone Weil never develops this thought in the way Wittgenstein does. But in her *Notebooks* she does return again and again to the question of what it is for human beings to understand one another and of the conditions under which such an understanding is possible. And by the time she came to write *The Need for Roots* towards the end of her life she had adopted a very different point of departure from what we find in *Lectures on Philosophy*. The fundamental notion of 'rootedness' is there explained as a '*real, active and natural participation in the life of a community* [my emphasis] which preserves in living shape certain particular treasures of the past and certain particular expectations for the future'. What is significant here is the merging of 'activity' with 'participation', which brings with it the possibility, lacking in *Lectures on Philosophy*, of integrating the idea that an individual's concepts are

---

[1] *Oppression and Liberty*, trans. Arthur Wills and John Petrie (Routledge & Kegan Paul, London 1958), p. 96.

a cultural heritage with the stress on his activity in his developing grasp of those concepts.

A shift in political perspective goes along with this shift in epistemological perspective. Obedience to the authority of other men is no longer seen as a social evil, however, unavoidable. On the contrary, it is listed in *The Need for Roots* as a 'need of the soul' along with liberty. Correspondingly, the problem of minimising oppression is now treated not as one of eliminating, as far as possible, subordination to authority, but rather, in one of its aspects, as one of ensuring that 'obedience' shall be consented to and not imposed by *force majeure*. This thought is beautifully developed in 'Human Personality'[1] and also in '*Luttons-nous pour la justice?* '.[2] Consent is only possible where there is mutual understanding and this is made possible by the necessary dependence of thinking individuals on the cultural heritage into which they grow. Consent takes different forms, is differently expressed, according to the specific social and political institutions within which it is exercised; and it is an illusion of perspective to suppose that, for instance, the consent necessary for a political regime to acquire legitimacy is to be found only within the context of parliamentary democracy – or even that the existence of such a context guarantees the presence of such consent. Human collectivities are the bearers of the symbolic forms of expression which make mutual understanding possible; Simone Weil thinks of them now as 'vital media' membership of which essentially involves forms of 'obedience', in the absence of which mutual understanding would hardly be conceivable. (This point is much illuminated by some of the things Wittgenstein has to say on the subject of 'training' and on what is involved in the acquisition of a *Weltbild* in his *On Certainty*.) It is part of the same shift in Simone Weil's perspective that, in *The Need for Roots*, there is much less emphasis on the *instrumental* character of human thought and action, as directed towards the realisation of projects, than there is in *Lectures on Philosophy*; and much more emphasis on their *expressive* character in relation to ideals of the good, the grasp of

[1] *Selected Essays*, trans. Richard Rees (Oxford University Press, 1962).
[2] In *Ecrits de Londres*.

which requires a symbolism which only the culture of historically specific human communities can provide.

Chapter 4, on morality, is devoted mainly to exposition and discussion of the work of other philosophers. Simone Weil's own distinctive contribution to moral philosophy was to be developed, at a later stage, mainly in the context of her religious thinking. Perhaps the most striking feature of this later development is the highly original way in which her treatment of ethical ideas is interwoven with topics usually regarded as quite distinct, such as the nature of scientific understanding. There are already indications of this approach in comments she makes about science in the *Lectures*, but it can be seen at a much more fully worked out stage in, for instance, the essays collected in *On Science, Necessity and the Love of God*.

Appended to the *Lectures* is a miscellany of suggested essay subjects for her students, together with sketches of possible treatments of those subjects. They do not seem to be arranged in any particular order, but most of them relate to discussions to be found in various parts of the *Lectures*.

I hope that the availability of Hugh Price's translation will help to make clearer the hard and systematic philosophical thinking out of which grew the characteristic ideas in her later writings which have justly attracted so much attention. But the *Lectures on Philosophy* are certainly worth study in their own right by anyone interested in fundamental philosophical questions. Teachers of philosophy, moreover, may find this a useful book with which to introduce students to those questions. Finding a suitable text for this purpose is a perennial problem: it must be accessible to those who are approaching the subject for the first time, but it must also convey the depth and seriousness of philosophical issues. 'Textbooks' of philosophy, specially written for teaching purposes usually have something second-hand about them which fails to meet that second requirement. The freshness and boldness of this book, along with its accessibility to anyone who is prepared to think for himself about the issues it raises, seem to me to make it in many ways ideal as an introduction to philosophy. It could very usefully be used alongside, say, that valuable old war-horse, Bertrand

Russell's *Problems of Philosophy*, treating as it does much the same
sort of question from such a very different point of view.

Bibliographical note

A volume containing essays which take further some of the ideas
in theory of knowledge and philosophy of science discussed in the
Lectures on Philosophy is:
On Science, Necessity and the Love of God, collected, translated, and
edited by Richard Rees (Oxford University Press 1968). This
includes material from: *Sur la science* (Gallimard, Paris 1965), and
along with other essays, some discussions of Greek Philosophy
from: *La source grecque* (Gallimard, Paris 1953). (Readers of *La
source grecque* should not miss the superb essay, 'L'Iliade, poème
de la force'.)

There are also some interesting discussions of mathematics and
science in: *Seventy Letters* translated and arranged by Richard Rees
(Oxford University Press 1965).

Those interested in Simone Weil's social and political ideas
should read: *Oppression et liberté* (Gallimard, Paris 1955) [*Oppres-
sion and Liberty*, translated by Arthur F. Wills and John Petrie
(Routledge & Kegan Paul, London 1958)] and: *L'enracinement*
(Gallimard, Paris 1949) [*The Need for Roots*, translated by Arthur
F. Wills and John Petrie (Routledge & Kegan Paul, London 1952)].

There are also some important essays on politics in: *Ecrits de
Londres* (Gallimard, Paris 1957). Particularly recommended in this
volume are the essays, 'La personne et le sacré', 'Luttons-nous
pour la justice?' and 'La légitimité du gouvernement provisoire'.
'La personne et le sacré' is included, under the title 'Human
Personality' in: *Selected Essays* 1934–43, chosen and translated by
Richard Rees (Oxford University Press 1962).

Simone Weil's religious ideas cannot really be separated from
the rest of her work; but anyone for whom these are of primary
interest should read: *L'attente de Dieu* (Fayard, Paris 1966) [*Waiting
on God*, translated by Emma Crauford (Fontana Books, London
1959)] and: *La pesanteur et la grace* (La Guilde du Livre, Lausanne
1964) [*Gravity and Grace*, translated by Arthur F. Wills (Routledge
& Kegan Paul, London 1952)]. *Gravity and Grace* consists of ex-

tracts from Simone Weil's notebooks, which are available in full as follows: *Cahiers* (2 vols, Plon, Paris 1970 and 1972) *La connaissance surnaturelle* (Gallimard, Paris 1950) [*First and Last Notebooks*, translated by Richard Rees (Oxford University Press, 1970); *The Notebooks of Simone Weil*, translated by Arthur F. Wills (2 vols, Routledge & Kegan Paul, London 1956)].

Readers in search of further material should consult: *Simone Weil, a Bibliography*, by J. P. Little, Grant & Cutler, 1973. This also lists a great deal of secondary material. There is a thoughtful assessment of Simone Weil's work by Gustave Thibon in: *Simone Weil telle que nous l'avons connue*, by J.-M. Perrin and Gustave Thibon (Fayard, Paris 1967).

The fullest biographical study is: *La vie de Simone Weil* (2 vols.) by Simone Pétrement (Fayard, Paris 1973) [*Simone Weil: A Life*, by Simone Pétrement, translated by Raymond Rosenthal (Mowbray, London 1977)].

I am very grateful to the Leverhulme Foundation for making it possible for me to work on Simone Weil's philosophy during the academic year 1976–7.

Peter Winch

Simone Weil is by now already well known and is portrayed by some as 'the greatest mystic of the century' and by others as 'a revolutionary anarchist'. So I thought it would be of interest to introduce her, quite simply, as a teacher of philosophy.

She taught me at the girls' secondary school at Roanne during the school year 1933–4. Our class was a small one and had a family atmosphere about it: housed apart from the main school buildings, in a little summer house almost lost in the school grounds, we made our first acquaintance with great thoughts in an atmosphere of complete independence. When the weather was good we had our lessons under the shade of a fine cedar tree, and sometimes they became a search for the solution to a problem in geometry, or a friendly conversation.

I could waste time by reminiscing at some length about some strange rows that took place: the headmistress coming to look for marks and positions which Simone Weil usually refused to give; our orders to rub out the platonic inscription we had written above our classroom door: 'No one admitted unless he knows geometry'.

But I share the distaste of Gustave Thibon for such reminiscences: like him, 'I loved her too much for that'.

If 'a brother cannot speak of his sister as a writer can about a fellow writer', neither can a pupil speak in that way of a teacher she admired so much and who has had such a profound influence on her.

One must aim higher than that. Long before she became famous, I had carefully kept all my notes of her lessons. Simone Weil was too straightforward, too honest to 'cram us for exams' in lessons, and keep her real thinking for other times. These notes of her lectures which are, I believe, very revelatory of her thinking at that time, are published here, with very little editing, more or less as they were written down by a seventeen-year-old adolescent. I hope the reader will excuse the carelessness and error he will undoubtedly find in them; let him regard them as marks of their authenticity. Anyone who has taken down notes in a classroom or lecture hall will know what their shortcomings must be; in a spoken lecture, a word, an inflection of the voice, or a smile can often modify a too categorical statement; all such nuances are lost in a hastily written transcript. Above all, it is important to stress that Simone Weil never dictated notes, and that my notes are not a verbatim transcript. *So these published notebooks are not a text produced by Simone Weil,* and one might be mistaken in attributing to her some remark taken out of its context. But at least I hope that the notes, taken as a whole, present a faithful reflection of her thought. I prefer not to burden them with comments of my own. I think they will speak for themselves and that through them the reader will be able to discern how far the thinking of the 'anarchist' was simply an inner discipline, a search for truth.

In doing this, I have once more re-lived a year with Simone Weil. Now I am about to reveal to the public an aspect, perhaps an unexpected one, of the young philosopher, by now entered into eternity, I think I can declare that there are not 'two Simone Weils' as people are beginning to say. And that is why I have stifled my scruples, although at first I was afraid of shocking people. (People do not like to be suddenly presented with an image of an artist, writer, hero or saint which is quite different from the one they had previously formed in their minds.) My scruples were vain. The Christian (by instinct if not by baptism) who, in 1943, died in a London hospital because she would not eat 'more than her ration', was the same person I had known, sharing her salary in 1933 with the factory-workers of Roanne.

The same person, too, were the mystic putting the 'void' before the 'real' (the well-known call, as she put it, of the 'void' for grace), and the physicist who, when speaking to us of 'verification' humbly allowed the facts to speak for themselves.

More than that: the nameless worker in the Renault factory (or the farm-girl in the Provençal countryside) was none other than the philosopher, so full of the intellectual pride (so it was said) of a disciple of Alain; but that philosopher already knew that 'pride can be used to bring about humility'.

By nature proud, she certainly struggled all her life against this tendency. In all her 'lessons' as in all her 'thoughts' there is the ever-recurring idea that there are 'truths one must not seek to understand', that one should not, indeed cannot do good consciously, that all value and all virtue cannot, of their very essence, be understood as such: her intelligence taught her that.

It was the same person, too, who in London forgot both work and meditation to tell stories to her landlady's retarded child (as Father Perrin related in his preface to *Waiting on God*) – and who in her philosophy lessons, when talking of 'sacrifice' warned us against self-denial and self-effacement. She was afraid of 'efforts which have the opposite effect to that desired (e.g. certain acts of devotion)' (*Gravity and Grace*, p. 106).

A careful study of the 'two Simone Weils' will thus reveal sometimes a development or a shift of thought, and sometimes apparent contradictions at which one will soon cease to be surprised; underlying all this there is a profound unity.

If it is true that 'he who acts truthfully finds the light', she certainly found the light. Her whole life was an illustration of those words of Goethe which she loved to quote and which we once used as a conclusion to some piece of work: 'Action is easy, thought is difficult; to reconcile action and thought is the most difficult of all.' She was not afraid of difficult tasks, and did not realise that she was accomplishing them.

May 1951   Anne Reynaud

1

The materialist point of view

'We should allow what is vile
in us to find its own level,
so that what is noble and fine
can rise upwards.'
(Simone Weil, *Gravity and Grace*)

Method in psychology

I *Study of the ways in which thought in other people shows itself* (objective psychology). Actions: reflex (from an external point of view everything is at the level of reflexes), custom, habit, voluntary actions.

II *Study of oneself* (introspection).

A. Introspection is a particular psychological state, incompatible with other psychological states.

1. With thinking about the world (astronomy, physics) and with theoretical speculation (mathematical reasoning).

2. With action, at least with voluntary action, for some involuntary actions do not exclude observations of oneself. But all actions which demand attention (sport, art, work) are incompatible with introspection. For example, the voluntary actions of Corneille's[1] heroes are incompatible with introspection: if Rodrigue had analysed his state of mind after he had learned of the way his father had been insulted, he would have seen there nothing but despair, and he would have done nothing.

3. With a very strong emotion.

---

[1] Pierre Corneille (1606–84). Rodrigue, a character in his play *Le Cid* (1636), is in love with Chimène, but is forced by the accepted code of honour of the time (sixteenth-century Spain) to kill her father who has insulted his, after Chimène's father has been appointed as a tutor by the king, a post Rodrigue's father had expected himself. Chimène, in her turn, demands her lover's (Rodrigue's) death – again as a matter of honour. He agrees to this and kills himself. *Le Cid*, trans. J. C. Lapp (Appleton-Century-Crofts, New York 1955).

Examples: love at first sight in Racine's *Phaedra*,[1] fear, deep joy, anger etc.

To sum up, thought, action, emotion exclude examination of oneself. Whenever, in life, one is actively involved in something, or one suffers violently, one cannot think about oneself.

Conclusion: since almost everything escapes self-observation, one cannot draw general conclusions from introspection. And it is not surprising that introspection should result in one's taking notice, for the most part, of what is passive in human thought (Amiel,[2] for example). By the very fact that one keeps a watch on oneself, one changes; and the change is for the worse since we prevent that which is of greatest value in us from playing its part.

B. Now that we have isolated introspection, let us examine it in itself.

Only states of mind then, can be the object of introspection – excluding, that is, violent emotions.

An experiment will show us that introspection, pushed to its very limits and applied in the present, defeats its own object: so that, if one tries to observe oneself in the present one finds in oneself only the state of observing oneself. Introspection, then, can only work in the case of past states of mind, and this does away with its objective validity for one can be mistaken about one's state of

---

[1] Jean Racine (1639–99). His play *Phèdre* is based on the classical Greek story of Phaedra and Hippolytus. (See Robert Graves, *The Greek Myths*, 2 vols, Penguin, Harmondsworth 1969, Vol. I, pp. 356 ff.) The story is the theme of Euripides's play *Hippolytus*. In Racine's play Phaedra is in love with Hippolytus who does not return her love; she poisons herself in her despair. *Phaedra*, translated into verse by Robert Lowell (Faber & Faber, London 1971).

[2] Henri F. Amiel (1821–81), professor of philosophy in Geneva, whose *Fragment d'un journal intime* is only part of a large manuscript of 17,000 pages. See for example p. 126 of the English translation by Mrs Humphry Ward (Macmillan & Co., London 1889). 'To arrive at a faithful portrait, succession must be converted into simultaneousness, plurality into unity, and all the changing phenomena must be traced back to their essence. There are ten men in me, according to time, place, surrounding and occasion; and in their restless diversity I am for ever escaping myself. Therefore, whatever I may reveal of my past, of my Journal, or of myself, is of no use to him who is without poetic intuition, and cannot recompose me as a whole, with or in spite of the elements which I confide to him.'

mind at some precise moment in one's past life. (For example: when one feels a lot of affection for someone one can forget that the first impression one had was quite the opposite.) Past feelings no longer exist unless they have been changed into actions. The object of introspection vanishes.

After examining the two methods used in psychology we see that:

1. if we examine other people, we are unable to determine the nature of their actions;

2. if one wants to direct one's thought on oneself one only sees one's own thought.

What answer is there to the problem?

Philosophers have found quite a number. Let us note:

1. The psychology of behaviour or 'behaviourism' (Watson[1]): everything is reduced to the level of a simple reflex. This answer amounts to saying: we cannot discover the soul, it does not exist.

2. The psychology of intuition (Bergson[2]): if we are unable to make our own states of mind an object of thought, if we have this feeling of there being nothing there, the reason for this is that intelligence is inadequate for the purpose. One has to depend on intuition. Intelligence has a social and practical end, but it does not enable us to dig down into our own natures. If one wants to get hold of thought, intelligence will be of no use to us.

The first solution gives no place to the soul; the second none to intelligence, though it does this in order to study the soul. For the first of these philosophers there are only states of body, and no states of mind. For Bergson it is not a matter of coming to know states of mind: what one has to do is to live them. These two theories are correlative to each other: they both suppress one of the terms of the contradiction one runs up against: the first is not psychological, the second is not scientific.

---

[1] John B. Watson (1878–1958), American psychologist; main work *Behaviourism* (New York 1925).

[2] Henri Bergson (1859–1941), French philosopher who was awarded the Nobel prize for literature in 1927. Among his better known works are *Creative Evolution*, trans. Arthur Mitchell (Macmillan & Co., London 1928), and *The Two Sources of Morality and Religion*, trans. R. A. Audra and C. Brereton (Macmillan & Co., London 1935).

Let us ask ourselves again: what answer is there to the problem?

We shall not try to put forward a scientific theory, but try to make an analysis. In any case, a scientific theory of thought is impossible, for thought serves as a means, and it is nothing at all except in so far as it is active; if one wants to observe it, it is no longer there, as we have already found out.

On the one hand we have the external world (the physical world), and on the other, the 'self' which is exactly what we have to study. Relations between the external world and the 'self':

We find nothing that is purely internal: in mathematical reasoning, for example, we need to have signs of some kind; while gaiety, sadness, depend on bodily conditions.

On the other hand, there is nothing which is purely external: the sensations produced by colours, for example, vary from person to person; impressions are subjective, each of us has his own view of the world.

We shall put forward the hypothesis that the external world really exists and we shall begin by studying the influence of the body on the soul.

Reflexes

It is, then, reflexes that the body gives us, that is to say reactions which are brought about by known stimuli.

A. First there are congenital reflexes (reflexes common to all normal people).

Examples: secretion of the digestive juices, movement of the leg when someone strikes it.

If we examine the relation between reactions and stimuli, we see that the latter are limitless in number, while the former are limited. The salivary gland, for example, always secretes saliva, whatever the food is. It is as if it were able to discern the general character of food throughout the infinite variety of foods. Other reflexes are more remarkable: the salivary glands secrete at the very sight of food, and yet the food never has the same look about it (change of colour, of shape).

So, by means of our reactions we generalise stimuli. If there were a different reaction corresponding to each stimulus, each reaction would only be produced once in a life time, and then life would be impossible.

It is in this way that the body classifies things in the world before there is any thought. (Example: the chick leaving the egg distinguishes between what is to be pecked and what not.)

So, from the very fact that we have a body, the world is ordered for it; it is arranged in order in relation to the body's reactions.

But there are not only congenital reflexes, because, in that case, the study of reflexes would be limited and could not be a part of psychology.

B. There are also acquired or conditioned reflexes.

Examples:

1. Pavlov's[1] experiment: he presented a dog with a piece of meat; the dog, of course, secreted saliva; then on a number of occasions he presented to the dog a piece of meat together with a red disc: the dog continued to secrete saliva; last of all, he presented the dog with nothing but the red disc: Pavlov discovered that the dog secreted saliva. This shows that a definite reaction, thanks to the simultaneity involved, can be produced by any stimulus whatsoever. The training of animals consists in their acquiring conditioned reflexes, by means of an association of ideas.

2. We can quite easily remind ourselves that if, for example, we have suffered in some place, then every time we go there again we experience real suffering.

3. Another example of an acquired reflex: a wooden chair or an armchair upholstered in velvet brings about the same reflex action in us: we get ready to sit down. And yet an armchair upholstered in velvet looks more like a table covered with the same velvet than like a wooden chair. So it is not our eyes that make this judgement.

Every thing that we see suggests some kind of movement, however imperceptible. (A chair suggests sitting down, stairs climbing up, etc.)

---

[1] Ivan Pavlov (1849–1936), Russian physiologist who was awarded the Nobel prize in 1904 for his work on digestive glands, and is best known for his work on conditioned reflexes. See his *Lectures on Conditioned Reflexes*, trans. W. Horsley Gantt (Martin Lawrence Ltd, London 1928).

It is, then, the things as a whole that have an affect on our bodies, and not their particular aspects. (The stairs can be made of wood or stone, covered with carpet or not, etc., they call up before anything else the idea of stairs.) What we are saying now has to do with something very important – the theory of forms (Gestalt theory[1]). German psychologists have made interesting experiments on this matter, which lead us to the conclusion that the body grasps relationships, and not the particular things. When one says that it is the relationships that make an impression on us, and that it is the things as a whole that do too, these two ideas are closely related one to the other. For example, someone makes a series of raps on the table: one can repeat the series without having counted them.

Thought does not come into these cases; it is the body which grasps the relations.

Conclusion of this study of reflexes:

Both congenital and acquired reflexes establish a classification among things in the world.

What makes an impression on the body are things as a whole and relations.

So, when we are on the point of giving birth to thought, it comes to birth in a world that already is ordered.

(Cf. Bergson: 'The idea of generality, at its root, is only our consciousness that we behave in the same way in different situations.'[2])

We are now going to have to investigate the extent to which reflexes play a part in human life; there is no doubt that this is a very large one. Education, for the most part, consists in providing children with conditioned reflexes. We mention too that we shall have to look into the question of whether all the moral ideas we have are nothing but conditioned reflexes (ideas of reward and punishment).

---

[1] Gestalt Theory. See G. Humphrey, *Thinking* (John Wiley & Sons, New York 1963), chapter 6, and W. Köhler, *Gestalt Psychology* (H. Liveright, New York 1929), also K. Koffka, *Principles of Gestalt Psychology* (Routledge & Kegan Paul, London and New York 1935).

[2] Bergson, *Creative Evolution*, chapter 3.

We can now draw out a general plan of our whole study.

A. *Role of the body* in: 1. action; 2. feeling; 3. thought.

B. *Role of the mind* in: 1. thought; 2. feeling; 3. action.

We are going to ask ourselves whether we can explain everything by means of the body, everything by means of the mind, or whether we have to bring in both of them. This question is really important, because morality, that is to say what governs and directs our life, will not be looked at in the same way in the three following cases:

For materialists, morality is only a matter of policy.

For idealists, morality is a matter of principles; as a result it becomes something that has no value.

For dualists, morality consists in putting matter under the control of mind.

Instinct

Among the reactions that are observed in living beings, there are some which are quite simple in nature, which are called reflexes (which we have already looked at) and others of a more complicated kind, which we call instincts. We have to find out whether instincts are in any way different from reflexes. This leads us to a complete theory of instincts.

Darwin's theory of instinct (Darwin – an English scientist of the nineteenth century).

It was Lamarck[1] who first spoke of evolution, but the theory is usually attributed to Darwin. It has given rise to disputes (people rejected it for religious reasons). In the middle of the nineteenth century there was a long drawn out discussion between the evolutionists (Lamarck and Geoffroy Sainte-Hilaire[2]) and the fixists (Cuvier[3]). The evolutionists won through. But what are the principles of evolution? According to Lamarck there are two which are the most important:

[1] Lamarck (1744–1829), French pioneer in biology, best known for his ideas about heredity which were criticised by Darwin.

[2] Geoffroy Saint-Hilaire (1772–1844), French naturalist who was a pioneer in the study of embryology.

[3] Georges Cuvier (1769–1832), French zoologist and palaeontologist, who was a pioneer in the study of comparative anatomy.

1. the effort to adapt oneself to the environment;

2. the inheritance of characteristics acquired by one's ancestors.

1. The effort to adapt oneself to the environment rests upon the instinct of self-preservation; so one of the fundamental instincts is defined as a cause. But how does one explain that itself?

Are instincts something different from a mechanism? According to Lamarck they are; for if it were just a case of a mechanism, an animal could just as well move to its own destruction. We also admit that instinct does not depend upon conscious thought. Here we refer to the studies that Fabre[1] has made on insects: for example, when a sphex stings a grub in its nerve centre, it is clear that this action would need more knowledge than a sphex could have.

2. One could say that action of this kind has been acquired by inheritance; that the ancestors of the sphex as it exists now have had to make many experiments in order to succeed in stinging the grub in its nerve centre. But a theory of this kind does not seem to be scientific: a highly gifted mathematician will not of necessity have children who are mathematicians.

So: principle 1 raises a question of method

principle 2 raises a question of fact.

They are hardly scientific, and that for different reasons.

Bergson gives an account of two ways of looking at life, depending on whether one is a mechanist or a finalist. But, according to Bergson, both these explanations are inadequate because each of them looks at life from the outside and not from within. He makes use of comparisons: the curve AB traced out by hand, iron filings which take the shape of a hand. (The life-force (*élan vital*) in his *Creative Evolution*.) In each of these examples the mechanist and the finalist do not see the thing from within. It is the same in the case of life: if one considers it from within, one sees a 'movement', a life-force – this is the source of the perfection which belongs to instincts. Darwin was a keen believer in the power of reason; he looked elsewhere.

If an animal were not adapted, it would die; a dead animal is

---

[1] Henri Fabre (1823–1915). French entymologist. See his *Book of Insects*, trans. Mrs Randolph Stawell (Tudor, New York 1921).

no longer an animal. Darwin thought therefore that adaptation was part of being an animal. So it is only a question of finding out how a successful adaptation comes about.

The fundamental idea of the elimination of beings that are not adapted is the beginning of a method of enquiry based on reason (the idea is already found among the ancients). But Darwin brought in another idea: that of the struggle for existence (the degree of adaptation depends on the degree of adaptation in others). So, due to the struggle for existence, it is not only those who are not adapted, but those who are less well adapted, who are eliminated. The best adapted animal has offspring; those offspring who survive are the best adapted ones, and these latter are better adapted than the parent animal. There is then, a mechanical progress, if we look at the matter purely from the point of view of appearances, and this is the result of the fact that everything which does not follow the line of progress is brutally eliminated. The proportion of those that are eliminated is, of course, large; the degree of perfection in the adaptive powers of those who survive is therefore very high. Only those beings survive who possess instincts, and instincts which have been perfected.

So: 1. spontaneous variation; 2. struggle for life; 3. natural selection.

In studying instinct we have to take account of the relation between structure and instinct. 'We are not able to say where organisation ends and instinct begins' (Bergson[1]).

Examples: the chick which breaks its shell, the bird which makes its nest. It is often difficult to distinguish instinct from structure. In the case of a bird there is, between the fact of digestion and that of making its nest, a series of facts intermediate between a function which is completely organic and instinct. There is nowhere a clear separation between them.

Take the flight of birds as an example. Is this an organic function or an instinct?

In the same way, there is only a difference of degree between a horse's ears twitching and its breaking into a gallop. If the horse

[1] Bergson, *Creative Evolution*, p. 174.

flies in the face of danger, one says that it does this instinctively: if its ears twitch, one says that this happens on account of organic structure. 'One can, as one pleases, say that instinct organises the means of which it is going to make use or that the organisation extends to the instinct which has determined the organ itself' (Bergson[1]).

(Bergson's view of the matter: he preferred to look at it in the first way, since organisation and instinct are for him two manifestations of the life-force, but he thought that instinct is movement, while organisation is a thing.)

Instinct gives the appearance of being knowledge that is limited to one single thing (the nerve centre in the case of the sphex, the hexagonal property in the case of bees). So, instinct cannot be knowledge, since knowledge is by its very nature something general.

To sum up: what is essential about 'Darwinism' is that it relates instinct to structure, and structure to the influence, whether it be direct or indirect, of the environment. The direct influence is brought about by spontaneous variations, the indirect influence by natural selection which is the result, in a general way, of the natural environment, and more particularly of the living environment.

Darwin does something like Descartes did in another sphere: he does away with hidden forces in animals. He thinks that, just as men make conscious choices, so nature's choices are made blindly.

Which solution shall we adopt? For the present, in studying this, we too shall reduce instinct to reflex action.

Let us now ask what place reflex action and instinct (that is to say the body) have in human life.

---

[1] This quotation from Bergson's *Creative Evolution*, for whatever reason, is not correct. What Bergson wrote should be translated as: 'One can, as one pleases, say that instinct organises the means of which it is going to make use or that the organisation extends to the instinct which must make use of the organ.' *Creative Evolution*, p. 147.

The role of the body in actions

Conditioned reflexes play a big part in our life (customs, family traditions, even in the smallest things, like the make of a product). One can ask oneself: aren't essentially moral ideas, like that of a lie, reflexes? Each word is for every man a conditioned reflex.

Work is based on conditioned reflexes: a mason, for example, has his attention drawn by a half-finished wall, a pianist by a piano. On the other hand, society has no end of means for creating conditioned reflexes: marks, positions, decorations.

To sum up: from outside it is impossible to say that an act of this kind is anything but a reflex.

The instinct of imitation is also an important factor in human actions.

The role of the body in feeling

I The mechanism of producing and reproducing feelings.

A. Filial instinct and maternal instinct.

There is a very strong bond between mother and child before birth, during childhood, and then for the rest of life.

One could say that at first, there is instinct and later conditioned reflex (on the part of the mother as well as the child). At first it is physiological: the need to suck, the need for suckling. Family relationships are knit together by the mother.

So it is very easy to explain family relationships by conditioned reflexes.

B. Sexual instinct.

This is more complicated. Freud studied the question.

1. The instinct in general: the change in character which comes with adolescence (cf. Byron's 'Don Juan') shows that it must be related to physiological change. Adolescence is the time when the possibility of experiencing all kinds of feelings appears: love, friendship, sympathy; it is the time when feelings for the family change; sometimes even there is a violent reaction set up (hate); if it is overcome, the relationships are restored once the crisis has passed; otherwise it reaches a breaking point.

A 'crisis' goes too with old age; the generosity of youth dies out in old age. So there is a relationship between feelings and physiological facts. One could say that in infancy, the vital energy of an animal is concentrated in the making of its natural tissues; then, when this is finished, the energy is devoted to the species. We may suppose that it is the same with human beings. What we still have to find out is how the vital energy available at the time of adolescence is redistributed. It is this that Freud studied. Did he come to any conclusion? In any case, it is certain that it is above all in emotions that physiological changes find expression at different stages in life.

2. From a more particular point of view (all this is much too general): if, for example, one wants to explain why such and such a young man falls in love with such and such a young woman one has to appeal to conditioned reflexes, if one is only studying physiological facts. 'We have been children before becoming men', said Descartes.[1] He thought of hate as the repetition of the physiological state in which the child was when it was given food which it disliked, anxiety as the repetition of the state in which the child was at the moment of birth, while everything that brings about a feeling of security is like an undisturbed, ideal pregnancy. As one goes on, the whole of human life reproduces these first moments. Descartes thought that whenever someone loves, he is in the same physiological state as he was in at the time when he was in his mother's arms. We still have to find out why these physiological states are reproduced: the first pleasure is that of sucking, the sight of the mother gives the child a feeling of pleasure; by a conditioned reflex, when he finds someone who reminds him of his mother, and therefore of a particular physiological state, he will feel love. And depending on the present physiological state and the sex of the object, it will be love in the strict sense of the word, or friendship, etc.

The love of Phaedra, for example, can be completely explained by reflex action: she loves Hippolytus because he reminds her of Theseus, but she hates him because the very word adultery arouses

---

[1] René Descartes (1596–1650). See *The Philosophical Works of Descartes*, trans. E. S. Haldane and G. R. T. Ross (Cambridge University Press, 1967), p. 391.

in her a reflex of horror. The two reflexes are contradictory; the situation is one she cannot get out of, it can only be resolved by death.

Stendhal too gives us good examples of the same kind of thing. (The case of Edward and the young girl who has seen a young man in church and taken him for the young man someone has spoken to her about. When the real Edward arrived on the scene, she no longer wanted to marry him.) It is a case of crystallisation: 'One only has to think of something perfect to see it in what one loves' (Stendhal, *De L'Amour*[1]). Spinoza:[2] 'Joy is the feeling of passing to a more perfect state, sorrow that of passing to a less perfect state.' 'Anything can, by accident, be the cause of joy or sorrow or desire.' 'Each time the soul is moved by two affections at the same time, then, in the future, every time it feels one of them again, it feels the other also...Everything which happens accidentally to the soul when it is in joy or in sorrow becomes afterwards, by accident, a cause of joy or of sorrow.'

So, by the very fact that one thing is like another which makes us feel joy or sadness, the first of them makes us feel joy or sorrow too.

II We have now to examine the nature of feeling itself.

Every violent emotion is accompanied by physical phenomena (fainting, tears). One might say that either these physical signs are the expression of a deep feeling or that these physical signs make up the feeling itself.

William James's way of putting it: 'One does not flee because one is afraid, one is afraid because one flees.'[3]

---

[1] Henri Stendhal (1783–1842) pseudonym for Marie Henri Beyle, French writer, whose writings are much more appreciated now than in his lifetime. One of his admirers was Balzac (see p. 194, note 2). See his *On Love*, trans. P. S. N. Wolff and C. N. S. Wolff (Duckworth & Co., London 1915), Bk 1, chapter 2: 'On the birth of love': 'I call "crystallization" that action of the mind which uses every opportunity to discover that the beloved object has previously unnoticed perfections.'

[2] Baruch Spinoza (1632–77), Jewish philosopher. See his *Ethics*, trans. A. E. Boyle (Everyman's Library), Part III, 'Concerning the origin and nature of the emotions', Prop. xv.

[3] William James (1842–1910), American psychologist and philosopher. See his *Principles of Psychology* (Macmillan & Co., London 1890), Vol. II, pp. 449 ff.

Let us examine this way of putting it by taking examples:

1. Someone who is learning to ride a bicycle is afraid of something in his way; he thinks only of avoiding it, but he thinks of it so much that his hands guide the handlebars straight in the direction of the obstacle. What is essential about this kind of happening is that the person riding the bicycle transfers into the object itself the resistance which his own body makes to what he wants to do. Let us call this transference into the object of that which is situated in the subject's body, imagination.

2. Fear of heights: the body feels as if it is falling, and giddiness can make it fall. Nymphs, naiads, etc. are the personification of danger, the imputing of a nemesis to the object itself. The object is indifferent to you, but you are not indifferent to the object; so you come to think that the object is not indifferent to you either.

3. Danger (herd of cows).

Conclusion: we shall say that the materialist theory of the life of the emotions is completely consistent; there are no contradictions in it; it rests on the following ideas:

The stuff of the feelings is made up of bodily movements (Wiliam James), and the bodily movements which make up feelings are all in fact either instincts, natural reflexes or conditioned reflexes, or a combination of all these (Descartes, Spinoza, Freud).

One must add that it is due to language that we are able to move from objects to feeling or vice versa, that signs are what prevent us from surrendering ourselves to pure phantasy.

The role of the body in thought

There are two things which show the influence of the body on thought: imagination and habit (= memory, when it is related to thought).

The more honestly we are materialists in this study we are making, the better we shall be able to defend ourselves against them later. So one could say that materialism and its opposite are correlative one to the other. It is by studying matter that we shall find mind.

The first thing that the body furnishes thought with is sensible appearance.

The senses and sensations: sight, touch etc.

1. Sight.

First attempt to find out what it is that sight teaches us about an object (chair):

(a) distinction between the chair and its surroundings; between the back, the seat, and the legs;

(b) the back: brown, with dark markings, light patches;

(c) the seat: like the back; (d) the legs: a number of them, length, darker in shade.

Discussion:

(a) Our eyes do not make the distinction.

(b) Do the eyes know the position of such and such a light patch? Do they at least know that it is in front of us? Surely not; our eyes have no knowledge of behind, so no more do they have knowledge of in front. Distance does not exist for sight; the eyes cannot take possession of their object (sight is the sense of admiration, as touch is that of possession.) (Cf. the poetry of Valéry on Narcissus[1], or the child who breaks a toy, in order to gain complete possession of it.) If we did away with distances, that would destroy our universe completely. Do all colours then exist in the same plane? One is tempted to believe this by analogy with pictures, mirrors. Where is this plane? Is it in front of us, or behind us? Wouldn't it change its position as we change ours? And what is there in front of and behind this plane? Could one even think of a plane without the idea of before, or behind? No. The idea of a plane implies the idea of a division of a space of three dimensions, the division between the two halves of this space divided by this plane, the equality of the distances beteween points situated on this plane and the corresponding points situated on parallel planes etc. Colours then do not exist on any plane. Space does not exist for sight.

(c) Do objects have a shape for sight? No: it is impossible to have the idea of shape without the idea of movement; a straight line or a curve is something which one scans (movement of the eyes, a finger, a pencil). The movement does not belong to the eyes.

[1] Paul Valéry (1871–1945), French poet. See *The Penguin Book of French Verse* (Harmondsworth, 1969), p. xxiv and pp. 541 ff.

(d) Is all that remains colours? But it is impossible to give a name to the colours one sees. Every coloured point has its own peculiar colour which is not like any other colour. Are there greater and lesser differences, for sight, between colours? The degrees of difference imply series which we have to construct and which we construct in our imaginations by making use of series which we can make from some material or other. Whenever there is a series, there is an activity of the mind. One could make series of colours (blue to red through violet) in such a way that it would be difficult to distinguish each term from those immediately next to it. So one cannot speak of series, nor of greater and lesser differences, by reference to sight alone. So long as two colours appear different, they are so absolutely. One does not lay down a series between the two, because one cannot order colours in a series except by relating them to quantities (an increasing proportion of blue). But as far as sight alone goes, there is no quantity. There is, properly speaking, no quantitative difference between qualities. The differences between qualities are differences of kind, not of degree. Series of qualities always depend on the conditions that produce the said qualities (cf. Bergson, *Essay*[1]). But the conditions for the production of a quality have nothing to do with the quality as far as its appearance goes.

So, each coloured point has its own colour which is not like any other, and each coloured point is completely changed from one moment to the next. There is, then, a diversity of an absolute kind in space and in time. Sight presents us with an aggregate which is infinitely diverse and changing. At any definite moment, sight teaches us nothing precise about the heterogeneous whole which it presents to us. We would then be able to say nothing about it if time were to stop. But time does not stop. We are hardly conscious of the aggregate of colours which sight presents to us, because this aggregate completely disappears and is replaced by another which has nothing in common with it and which in its turn disappears.

To conclude, sight by itself gives us nothing.

[1] Bergson, *Time and Free Will. An Essay on the Immediate Data of Consciousness*, trans. F. L. Pogson (G. Allen & Unwin, London 1910), pp. 50–4.

2. Touch (passive, that is without movement).

One can make the same analysis.

It provides us with neither distances nor shapes. Space does not exist for touch, in so far as it is passive, any more than it does for sight. The sensations which touch, in so far as it is passive, gives us (of hardness, roughness, cold, etc.) form an aggregate as completely mixed up together and as heterogeneous as that of colours.

Touch, as something passive, does not give us the position of objects. But, doesn't it at least give us the position of the body which we feel? The illusions of people with amputated limbs. Examples where one is in pain without knowing where. Pain of itself does not tell us where it comes from (the case of having pain in a healthy tooth when it is the one next to it that is bad). One assigns a place to the pain by moving or touching in turn a number of parts of the body. In itself, the pain is a pure quality, a state of mind which does not belong to any location.

So, touch provides us with sensations which are quite different as qualities, but which do not have location any more than those of sight do.

3. Hearing: the sound does not belong to the cause of sound. Sound has no position, any more than colour does, and it is only an object for the sense of hearing. Our ear cannot tell us where the sound comes from, for it does not even know whether the sound has a cause.

4. Smell: ⎫
5. Taste: ⎭ same analysis.

Conclusion about the senses: none of the senses tells us that there are other senses. None of the senses tells us how the sensations it gives are related to those that are given by the other senses. Sight tells us nothing about the eyes, not hearing about the ear, etc., since the senses work in a passive way.

What we can say about the operation of the senses apart from movement is that we have an infinite variety of sensations and that they teach us nothing at all.

The sense of movement

Sensations of touch are always made possible for us by movement – e.g. kinaesthetic sensations and sensations of pain. These involve some kind of change. But the change is qualitative, the movement quantitative. The problem is one of knowing how we are to move from a qualitative change to a quantitative movement which takes place in space.

The sensible changes which are perceived in movement still do not give us space: there is, for example, no space in pain; our pain, as a thought, extends throughout the world (if one looks at a fine landscape when one is in terrible pain one cannot admire it. The pain fills our whole universe; if, when one has toothache, the pain were to stay localised in the tooth, one could read, admire things, etc.). The kind of pain which movement brings with it is not any more localised. Touch does not give any sense of space. Sensations, which do not include space, change; but their doing so does not give us space.

One feels once the nerve-impulse is transmitted by the motor nerve. The feeling of the nerve-impulse would be that of bringing about a muscular effort.

Experiment: one can bring about the feeling of effort without making an effort. But it is the stopping breathing, the tension of the muscles which, in this case, gives the sensation of effort. Now, would it be possible, in a direct way, without anything intervening, to have a feeling of exertion? Does one feel exertion in so far as one is the cause of it or only in so far as one is subject to it? Do we feel only the results of our activity, or do we feel our activity itself? Do we, as a matter of habit, take the results for the activity itself? As in hearing we take the cause of the sound for the sound itself.

There is one thing that is certain: it is that we never feel pure activity; activity is inseparable from its results.

What is more, in nearly all cases, the feeling of effort is inversely proportional to its being voluntary: effortlessness is always a sign of a real exercise of the will. The man who knows how to do something (art, sport, work) does not give the impression of exerting himself (a tennis player, a harvester, etc.). The feeling of effort is a sign that the will is no longer at work (pain, emotion, clumsiness etc.). In tragedies, calm comes when the will is most active ('Let us be friends, Cinna...'[1]); so effortlessness is also the sign of heroism as it is of craftsmanship. The more pure the will is, the less effort there is. This leads us to think that effort is most often some kind of constraint.

In conclusion: sensation is always something one undergoes, something passive, even when one feels the will powerfully at work.

Moral significance: the illusion that one feels oneself making an effort is the source of the morality of mysticism, of pharisaism. Being straightforward consists in trying not to think that one is being virtuous. To believe that one feels one's own activity consists in feeling satisfied by this feeling: take for example those people who think themselves great artists on account of the unrealised ideas that they believe they have. Any fault amounts to being passive instead of being active. We only know our own action by its results.

Sensations and time

So, to feel is always to undergo something or other. The feeling by itself tells us absolutely nothing about the world or about ourselves. Sensations do not come to us at once as something definite. (Cf. Lagneau:[2] sensation is something abstract.) One cannot distinguish a sensation, until one has related it to an object. Condillac[3] (a materialist philosopher of the school of the British

---

[1] Corneille's (see p. 27, note 1) play *Cinna* (1640) was based on a passage of Seneca (*De Clementia*, I. ix) and deals with the clemency of the Emperor Augustus. The words of Augustus quoted here: 'Let us be friends, Cinna...' come in the last scene of the play (act V, scene iii).

[2] Jules Lagneau (1851–94), French philosopher who was influenced by Jules Lachelier (see p. 109, note 1). Alain, who taught Simone Weil philosophy, wrote *Souvenirs concernant Lagneau*, 1925.

[3] Condillac (1715–80), French philosopher who was influenced by the ideas of John Locke. He is said here to be a materialist philosopher; but Ueberweg says of him: 'Condillac is a sensationalist, but not a materialist. He holds it is not possible that matter should think and feel, since, as extended and divisible, it is an aggregation of parts, whereas feeling and

empiricists) had a theory that all thought is made up of sensations. Example: if one begins by ascribing a sense of smell to a statue, then, if one offers it a beautiful rose to smell, the statue, if it could speak, would say: 'I am the smell of a rose'. Whenever we limit ourselves to feelings, we are the aggregate of all experienced sensations.

Sensations then do not give us the idea of space. Do they give us that of time? A sensation is after all something that lasts, but for sensations to be able to give us the idea of time it would be necessary for us to be able to attach some significance to past sensations.

Let us take remembering music as an example. One begins by reproducing the melody; but we know that we do not succeed in reproducing the sensation; we then try to remind ourselves of the object which produced it or the impression that was made on us by this sensation.

Analysis of the memory of a sensation regarded as a pure quality (for example, the blueness of the sky one sees in dreaming, a note of a double-bass). We always try: 1. to reproduce or rediscover in the world something which resembles the past sensation; 2. to reproduce as faithfully as possible the reaction the sensation produced in us. As far as the sensation itself is concerned, one cannot think of it, except by actually feeling it. A past sensation, or one to come, is then absolutely nothing, and, as a result, since sensations have significance only in relation to the present moment, there is in them no passing of time and they do not give us the idea of time. It is difficult for us to believe that they do not give us the idea of time because they possess some kind of duration. But, in this case, one should call to mind Bergson's analysis and his distinction between time and duration. Time is something homogeneous and indefinite; duration is a single characteristic of the quality of a sensation. If we have the impression of duration in the case of a sensation, that only means that sensations are not brought about in an isolated way: there is a continuity, an overlapping of sensations. The duration of

thought imply the unity of the subject.' (*History of Philosophy* (Hodder & Stoughton, London 1872), Vol. II, p. 127).

sensations does not mean that they involve time. On the contrary, it is possible to limit sensations to the present moment; to say that sensations are limited to the present moment would be to locate them once again in time.

Conclusion about sensations in general:

Sensations tell us nothing about the world: they contain neither matter, space, time, and they give us nothing outside of themselves, and in a way they are nothing.

Nevertheless, we perceive the world; so what is given us is not simply sensations. Far from sensation being the only thing that is immediately given to us, it is, as such, only given to us by an effort of abstraction, and by a great effort at that.

Examples: impressionist painting, analyses of sensation. Sensations are not immediately given, just as they are, to consciousness, otherwise we should not have had to make such an effort to study sensations; the impressionist painters would not have had to go to so much trouble to reproduce what they saw; the paintings are presented to us as representations of things that have been imagined, which have no relation with sensation, but only with our reactions to sensations.

Perception

The role of the imagination in perception

The extent to which imagination alters sensations. Relation between imagination and pure appearance.

A. Can imagination alter sensation or take its place?

In the case of normal perception, it seems clear that imagination does not alter the normal sensation and that it cannot take its place. The same goes for illusion. In the case of dreaming, the matter is more complicated. It seems that then there might be imaginary sensations.

Let us look at it more closely.

Examples: a psychologist who studies dreams, dreams that he has been before a revolutionary tribunal and that he is on his way to be guillotined; he feels the cold blade of the guillotine, and at that moment, he wakes up. His wife has struck him on the neck.

What is strange is that the dream, which the subject seemed to think lasted a long time, took place in an instant, and that even the visions of the tribunal took place after the blow was struck.

Someone else has dreamed that he sees and hears a ghost dragging its chains; when he wakes up, he recognises the noise of the alarm clock.

It is certain that, during the night, we have very many sensations: auditory sensations (they have a great influence). Tactile sensations: of the weight and resistance of bedclothes, the sensations of the weight of the body, of the function of organs (the heart). Sensations of taste which last just as those of smell do. Sensations of sight (they last throughout the whole course of the night, the retina is always producing images).

Now to deal with illusions: the problem is that of knowing whether there is, between a dream and an illusion, a difference of degree or one of kind.

We can at least say this: the change from dreaming to being awake does not provide us with the sensations which already existed during the dream; and, after waking up, the illusions continue (for example one embroiders what is going on while one is awake instead of embroidering the dream). One could say that a dream is an illusion which brings in the whole of perception; a dream is not an hallucination (unreal sensations) but an illusion (the imagination added to sensations).

So, all sensations are really felt, and the imagination is never changed into sensations.

B. What is in the foreground of consciousness? Is it what is imagined or what is felt?

One is conscious of what one believes one sees, and not of what one sees, of what one believes one touches, and not of what one touches, etc. Sensation only serves as an occasion for becoming conscious of what one believes one feels.

Example: if one draws on a blackboard a white cube, then a pink one, we shall see hardly any difference between them; we shall always see a cube.

So one thinks of them as the same because there is a sameness in what one imagines and not in what one sees. The source of the identity of objects is in the imagination alone.

Let us look for everything that belongs to the external world that is given us through the imagination.

1. There is, in the first place, space.

Example of the drawn parallelepiped: one really sees something spatial. What is it that causes this impression of space? One might think that this imaginary cube is perceived in analogy with a real cube; but we have never seen a real cube. Cubic space is really the result of the gesture of grasping the object. The space which we imagine the cube to fill is essentially a relationship between sensations and myself, and consists of a disposition to act in a certain way. Is there any difference between imaginary space and real space? If we consider only the relationship there is between the way we see the drawn cube and the way we see the real one, we see that there is no real difference between them at all. The spatial relations, of whatever kind they may be, are always made up of a relationship between ourselves and sensations, and these relationships are really a disposition to act in a certain way, which is brought about in us by the sensations.

When one sees a mirror, one wants to go towards it; one only stops once one knows that it is a mirror. All spaces, even those over which we do not in fact travel, make us want to do so. The attraction of architecture depends on this natural tendency (cathedrals, great staircases), the attraction of natural scenery: one feels stifled in a narrow valley, and this feeling does not occur in open country, even if one does not move about in it; one feels rested in secluded places, but one does not feel like this in wide open spaces, even if one is sitting down; the reason for this is that one wants to travel over its whole expanse.

2. Relief.

The phenomenon of red and green spectacles and the geometry of space. Stereoscopes.

In both cases, one believes one sees in relief what is flat – and one thinks one sees one image where, in fact, there are two. Can we say that these illusions come about in a way analogous to real perception? In fact each of our eyes has an image of its own,

neither of which we see. (What is necessary, in the first place, for
double vision to take place, is to be motionless.) The two images
follow one another at equal intervals; the images are different, but
the effect of our movement on each image is the same. Our body
has then a natural tendency to treat two visual images as if they
were only one. (Cf. when one takes hold of the two ends of a book,
the two hands come into action of necessity at the same time, and
it is in relation to one's carrying the book that it is one thing.) As
long as the eyes do not move, one has no reason to believe that
it is the same object, but when the eyes convey what they see, they
become aware of the unity of the object.

So, once again, what I think I see is not what I see, but rather
what corresponds to my bodily reactions.

Another example: Descartes compares sight to a blind's man's
stick; instead of thinking that there is a small man in the brain
who sees the retinal images, it is better to think of the eyes as two
sticks belonging to a blind man (and with his two sticks, the blind
man is able to ascertain through movement whether he has to do
with a single object or with two different ones).

So the visual depth of external objects is as illusory as the depth
of an image seen with a stereoscope. Nor do we have to say that
there are really two flat images for each object; they are flat only
in the retina, and, besides, if one sees them, the sense of the
reality of the object is lost too.

3. Shape.

Example: take the lamp on the ceiling. We say that it is circular
in shape. Should we say: the perception of a circle is imaginary;
we really see an ellipse?

The ellipse is certainly on our retina, but we have never seen
it there and there is no small man in our brain. Moreover, the
ellipse which one believes one sees is not identical with either of
those which each of our eyes sees.

In the second place, in order to see the lamp as an ellipse, one
has to see it in isolation from the ceiling, otherwise one could not
consider it as a unity. When one moves one's eyes the image
disappears more quickly than the background; it is this that gives
a unity to the object.

From the successive images of the lamp, we choose one which is not more real than any of the others. So, one cannot say: I believe I see a circle, but I see an ellipse, for the ellipse and the circle are completely correlative to each other: once one loses the idea of the ellipse, one loses that of the circle as well.

Objects assume a shape only through our imagining what we call their real shape. We call the real shape the shape which appears to us when the object occupies the whole of our visual field. One can ask: what reasons are there which make us decide the matter in this way?

Some other considerations: it is impossible to see two or three points at the same time; one brings them together to make of them a segment of a straight line, a triangle. Now, this triangle does not exist; what exists are three points, and that is all. The imagination is at work.

Let us ask ourselves why we are unable to see three points, but a triangle. The triangle is traced out by our looking, I add nothing if I draw in the lines. To think of two points is to think of a straight line. To think of a point is to think of the straight line which connects us to it. One can extend this to all the things that surround us. All the lines which form the limits of things, which make up their shapes, are given to us through our reflexes, by our own movement.

So, space, depth, shapes are given to us by our imagination. We must not forget, in this case, that 'imagination' should not be taken as something completely synonymous with fantasy or as something arbitrary: when we see two points we are not free to see anything else except a straight line.

There is already, then, an elementary geometry in perception. Everything happens as if our bodies already knew the geometrical theorems which our mind does not yet know.

There is already geometry in normal perception. So we should not be surprised if there is imagination at work in geometry, since it is already at work in perception. (We shall deal with this question when we consider geometry.)

It is the same cause really (imagination) which enables us to perceive the most ordinary things, and do geometry, which is at the foundation of all the sciences; it is this too which moves us in a cathedral spire or in a symphony (cf. Paul Valéry, in *Eupalinos*[1]).

The very nature of the relationship between ourselves and what is external to us, a relationship which consists in a reaction, a reflex, is our perception of the external world. Perception of nature, pure and simple, is a sort of dance; it is this dance that makes perception possible for us.

4. The imagination also plays a part in sensations which are not felt: when we see something we do not think so much of a colour, but of a weight, a consistency, etc.

If we glance at a book we can say that it is a book, that we turn over the pages, that it is made of paper, etc.

In the same way, if our hand bumps against something that has an angle, we will say that we feel the corner of a table that has the shape of a rectangle, but we will not necessarily remember what we felt. If we are very thirsty, and we see something that looks like water, the appearance of water speaks much more to our throats than to our eyes. We can analyse any perception whatsoever in this way.

So what affects one sense speaks to other senses too.

5. Illusions arising from movement (cinema, waves of the sea, rivers, the moon at the horizon) and illusions about the size of things are quite obscure. For all that, something vertical does not appear to have the same length as something horizontal. For the most part it is astonishment and surprise that seems to add to the size.

6. The identity of objects.

We think of the individual separateness of things in analogy with the individuality of other human beings to whom we ascribe a soul in analogy with ourselves.

Our first idea of unity comes from ourselves. The idea of mutilation, which goes together with that of unity, has a sense in the first place in the case of human beings and then for manufactured objects, animals, plants. Finally, minerals seem to have

[1] See p. 41, note 1. Valéry's *Eupalinos or the Architect* is a dialogue between Socrates and Phaedrus on questions relating to art, trans. W. C. Stewart (Oxford University Press, London 1932).

a unity in analogy with things that are manufactured. (Example: sand does not have any unity about it, but a heap of sand does because it seems to have been made. The same applies to liquids.)

Just as we refer all the senses to ourselves (as individuals), so we refer all sensations to the same object. The mental form of the object seems to us to derive from a grouping together of these sensations. To all intents and purposes, it is the aggregate of reactions which I have face to face with an object which creates its unity.

The individualness of each thing derives from the particular attitude we have when we are face to face with this thing. Through movements, I am aware that all sensations coalesce to give me a certain impression which explains the reaction and it is this impression which gives me the idea of the object's unity. All notions of coming together and separation come into being on account of movement.

7. Distinction between the essential and accidental properties of an object.

Some sensations seem to us to express essential properties, others accidental ones.

Example: a book is yellow; a shadow is cast on it: one sees something grey, but that seems accidental to us, it seems to us that there is, underneath, a layer of yellow. Now, the yellow and grey are really nowhere. The colours, which I change at will, seem to us to be simply superimposed on the object. I can cast a shadow on the object at will. It takes an effort to sustain the colour grey.

One can give the same analysis for sound, touch, etc. All this gives us a very good idea of the very important part which imagination plays in perception.

The role of the memory in perception

N.B. To discuss the role of the memory in perception is to discuss the role of the imagination, with the following differences – that one relates the reactions produced by an object to past reactions.

Examples: Odysseus's bow[1]; his fingers feel it again, the bow is bent (in the Odyssey).

Proust's analysis: he returns from a walk, he is very tired; his tiredness disappears once he sees his house.

Bergson's analysis: a village one knows well seems completely different from one one does not know at all. We have often had this experience.

Kipling: *The man who was*[2]: a passage in which, in India, a man causes surprise when he breaks his glass after he has drunk the queen's health, and by reacting in an unusual way. His body had recognised his company, but his mind had not yet done so. In fact, it was found out after some enquiry that an officer had disappeared thirteen years before from this very company.

Making a mistake in recognising something: if the body is perfectly happy with something (as Odysseus is with his bow) one has the impression that one has to do with something quite familiar. This only goes to show that everything is a result of the way we react.

Recollection: in the case of recollection one locates the object in time, while memory is made up simply of traces of the past, without relating the object to some definite moment in the past. Example: we have memory in the case of a schoolchild who knows some poetry; there is recollection if a schoolchild knows that he recited the poetry in such and such circumstances. (Cf. Bergson: 'The past continues to exist in two quite distinct ways: 1. in motor reactions; 2. in individual acts of recollection.'[3])

We shall look at individual acts of recollection and for the time being we shall, of course, discuss it from a materialist point of view.

Bergson: 'Memory which does nothing but bring into operation in the present things remembered from the past has all the characteristics of a habit (for example, a lesson learnt off by heart).

[1] See Homer's *Odyssey*, Bk 21.
[2] Rudyard Kipling (1865–1936), English writer born in Bombay, India, who won the Nobel prize for literature in 1907. See Kipling's *Life's Handicap* (Macmillan & Co., London 1897), p. 96.
[3] Bergson, *Matter and Memory*, trans. N. M. Paul and W. S. Palmer (Sonnenschein & Co., New York 1911), chapter 2, p. 87.

The recollection of something that has happened and which one associates with a definite time in the past, has none of the marks of habit'[1] (what has happened has happened only once, and cannot be repeated). Recollection is related to feeling, not to usefulness (for example, we will recall the important dates in the life of someone who is a hero of ours and whom we love more easily than a set of historical dates that are useful for an examination). And, yet, we have said that no traces of states of mind are left in us. This is not really a contradiction. For example, let us suppose that at some moment or other a new way of looking at something is opened up for us: at that moment we are drawn towards the future (this often happens in adolescence: the discovery of a skill, etc.).

Bergson refers memory which takes place automatically to the body alone, and recollections only to thought. The main feature of recollection is that it is complete all at once; time can add nothing to it: it can do nothing except blot it out. A lesson which is repeated, however, will be all the better known for that. Mechanical memory is of such a kind that it comes under the influence of the will, while recollection is involuntary. Recollection has to do with what is past and gone. So it looks as if thought of the past as such cannot be reduced to a reflex.

Bergson's theory: there is an unconscious where recollections are stored. But we cannot call to mind all our recollections at once; we cannot, for example, at the same time call to mind a moment of anger and one of calm, and the reason for this is that the present states of the body corresponding to these feelings exclude one another. The body would react in a negative way. All the time, all the reactions which our bodily state does not exclude enter into our minds. Recollections become conscious once they are brought into play by the body.

This is an ingenious and attractive theory, but it does not seem to be very scientific: what is this unconscious? Is a recollection which does not exist anything at all? There are feelings which do not have anything, in the world of the present, as their object, and

---

[1] *Ibid.*, pp. 89–90. This quotation as given in the notes is part quotation and part explanation, but does agree with what Bergson wrote.

which will continue to be unexpressed, which will never emerge from the unconscious.

We seem to have discovered mind in recollection. Let us look at these things more closely.

Analysis of recollection:

Proust: the cup of tea and the little cake.[1]

A powerful feeling which goes far beyond its object. This change comes about in him unconsciously, we may even say mechanically.

By emptying his mind Proust has the impression that this feeling has some effect on him, but he doesn't know what. Then, all of a sudden, the recollection comes to him.

The more searching Proust does, the more the recollection escapes him and is not recalled. So the mind plays no part in recollection taking place.

The taste of the little cake dipped in the tea does not bear any date in itself; it brings back the past only when the taste of the little cake makes him recall something which no longer exists in the present. An association of this kind is very largely explained as a conditioned reflex.

The process of recollection:

1. There are perceptions which bring with them feelings which are out of all proportion to the immediate perception itself (joy and sorrow). In all these cases, the feeling comes before the idea of its cause (as when one wakes up all tensed up without knowing the reason for it – or when one sees again a place where one suffered and the suffering begins all over again without one's knowing why).

2. Objects arouse attitudes, emotions which have nothing to do with what one is looking at at the time, but which bring to mind other things (for Proust: his aunt, Combray,[2] his childhood). It so happens that these other things have a definite time attached to

[1] Marcel Proust (1871–1922). See his *Remembrance of Things Past*, trans. C. K. Scott Moncrieff (Chatto & Windus, London 1941), Vol. I, pp. 58 ff.

[2] Combray is the name which Proust gave to Illiers, the small French town where his father was born, and where, until he was eighteen, Proust used to spend his holidays at the home of his aunt, Madame Amiot, the 'aunt Leonie' of his novel. This house is now a Proust museum, and is

them. The recollection of each of them, through the things that bring them to mind, brings with it a remembrance of the time each happened. (Family conversations: 'It was the year when so-and-so was married, when someone else was ill, etc.') No mental effort of ours can give a definite date to recollections unless there is something about them which enables us to give them a definite date. If recollections did depend on the mind, it would not be possible to have recollections scattered over a long period of time, about which one doesn't know whether they are things which one has lived through or dreamt.

Besides, we call things which date an event 'souvenirs'. So, it is in this way that we commonly think of perception as having a powerful influence. (Cf. family souvenirs, wedding rings, the handkerchief in *Othello*.) Things are means of bringing something to mind; we need things which have no value in themselves to remind ourselves of those whom we love the most. Things then take on a real power. Prisoners who possess nothing of this kind write the names of loved ones on the walls of their cells, lovers on the trunks of trees. One tries to create things which will be closely associated with one's own name in order to perpetuate one's own memory. It is matter and not mind which faithfully preserves memory. Every man's aspiration is to leave behind a memorial to himself enshrined in matter.

Study of what appear to be intellectual operations

General ideas

'Man', 'dog', 'being', 'red', etc., all these words express general ideas. There was a great deal of discussion about general ideas in medieval times.

Nominalist school: nothing exists except particular things.

Realist school: general ideas have real existence.

The nominalist school says: 'Where is the man who has neither dark eyes, blue eyes, brown eyes, etc., who has neither blond hair,

maintained by the Society of the Friends of Marcel Proust. It still contains the furniture as it was in Proust's childhood, and even an imitation madeleine (little cake) at the side of what was his aunt's bed.

red hair, or brown hair, etc.? Where is the triangle which is neither isoceles, scalene, equilateral, etc.'?

But the nominalist thesis is absurd, because one could just as well say: 'Mr X and a chair are as like one another as Mr X and Mr Z.'

It is, however, necessary that man exists in some way or other in order that one can have an idea of him. The relation between things and ourselves is determined by the reactions which things bring about in us. Man is above all the being to whom one speaks; the eyes are something into which one looks and which move as a result of one's looking at them, etc.

So, what there is in common between everything there is of the same kind, does not belong to the world but to our human body. (A child calls all men 'papa' at first.) Spinoza:[1] 'Terms such as "being", "things", etc. have their origin in the fact that the body, in so far as it is limited, is able to form in itself, in a definite way, only a limited number of images. ("Images" are the traces which things leave in the body, traces which in fact are the reactions of the body to things.) If this number is exceeded, these images begin to become confused; and if it is exceeded by a great deal, they become completely confused. If this happens, the mind will imagine all bodies as having nothing distinctive about them, and will bring them together somehow under a single attribute, say that of being, thing, etc. It is the same with the general ideas man, dog, etc. For human beings have such a vast number of images of men that their powers of imagination are overtaxed, not completely that is, but enough for them not to be able to imagine how many men there are and each one's particular features. One only has a definite image of that in which all men, in so far as they affect the body, are alike and it is this which in their case the name man expresses. This is why the name man does not mean the same thing for everyone.'

So, what is called a general idea is in fact simply a confused image. The mind always begins with this confused image, and only then goes on to have some specific idea.

[1] Spinoza, *Ethics*, Part II 'Concerning the Nature and Origin of the Mind', Prop. XL, note 1.

(Cf. Pascal:[1] 'The more the mind is at work, the more one sees what is original.')

Contrary to what is commonly believed, one moves from the general to the particular, from the abstract to the concrete. (This has important consequences for teaching.)

A work of art is something which is unlike anything else. It is art which, best of all, gives us the idea of what is particular. For example Notre Dame de Paris is Notre Dame, not just a church. A fine picture does not give us the idea of a picture in general. It is sacrilege to think so. And art has its origin in religion. It is due to religion and art that one can arrive at a representation of what is individual; it is due to feeling (friendship, love, affection) that one human being is different from others. To label, classify someone one loves, that is impious.

In order to make children observe, to make them pass from what is abstract to what is concrete, one has to appeal to feeling.

It is due to feeling alone that a thing becomes freed from abstraction and becomes something individual and concrete.

So, contrary to what is commonly believed, the contemplation of particular things is what elevates a man, and distinguishes him from animals. Animals never distinguish between an object and its utility. That is the reason why nothing individual and concrete exists for them; nothing particular exists as far as their bodies are concerned (wild animals).

Abstraction

The problem of abstraction is exactly the same as that of general ideas. We call what characterises general ideas abstract.

[1] This quotation from Pascal may be incorrect, and that the reference should be to the passage which is mentioned later (p. 201) where Simone Weil refers to the distinction Pascal makes between the kind of thought revealed in geometry and that revealed in shrewdness of mind. See Pascal, *Pensées*, section I, 7: 'A mesure qu'on a plus d'esprit on trouve qu'il y a plus d'hommes originaux. Les gens du commun ne trouvent pas de différence entre les hommes.' (The more intelligence one has, the more one sees what is original about people. Ordinary people do not see how different people are.)

Comparison

One might be tempted to believe that it is the mind alone which can construct relations. But here one must remember the case of the monkey who grasped relationships between colours. In our own case, we know that we do not see a white spot as pure white; but that it is more or less white in so far as it is surrounded by black or not; in the same way, a sound seems more or less loud in so far as it is heard at night when there is a deep silence, or during the day. Imagination works on relationships. We are aware that two objects are different in colour before we are aware of what each particular colour is. We move from the aggregate to the detail. For, the perception of the aggregate is the perception of relations. What is of importance, as far as the body is concerned, is the change which the thing produces in it. The attitude the body has in relation to a habitual noise is more or less the same as it is to silence. The body reacts in the same way to silence as to continuous noise: it reacts in the same way to a slight noise in the midst of silence as it does to a loud noise in the midst of continuous noise.

The reaction of the body brings about a relation between two things; it is the imagination which makes the relations.

Association of ideas

1. How it comes about:

Examples: (a) Proust's little cake; he remembers his aunt, and then the bedroom, then Combray etc. (contiguity).

(b) Going to bed brings to mind the drama of kissing his mother goodbye, the worries of childhood (resemblance). Other examples: a portrait brings to mind the person whose portrait it is; children who resemble their parents; Hippolytus is the image of Theseus for Phaedra.[1]

(c) Black makes one think of white, what is large of what is small (association through contrast).

2. Its importance:

[1] See p. 28, note 1. Theseus is Hippolytus's father, and Phaedra's husband, but Hippolytus's mother was Antiope.

The idea of the 'associationists', that all the operations of the mind can be reduced to the association of images.

Taine: 'The mind is a mass of images.'[1]

This is not a materialist theory; it leaves the body and all mental activity out of account. It is a theory which is purely psychological, which has nothing to do with an active self nor with bodily states.

Let us look at its different parts:

Day-dreaming: clearly associations play a role here.

Judgements: relations of time and space; relations of resemblance and difference.

One could think of these judgements as the expression of ideas which become stuck, as it were, the one to the other.

Scientific reasoning

Algebra: the mind has a natural tendency to bring similar terms together.

Geometry: the discovery of a theorem often comes because one is reminded of other theorems: one calls to mind the necessary theorems, the solutions that are given of similar questions.

Physics: the analogies between light and sound, between electricity and water: the theory of gravitation based on the analogy between falling bodies and the movement of the moon and planets. All the time one is thinking of natural forces as simple machines. All physical theory is based on an analogy that is made between things which are not well understood and things which are simple.

So one could say that what one takes to be the activity of human thought is nothing but a conglomeration of representations.

This is the theory of psychological atomism. Those who hold it think that it is possible to have a real science of the mind.

[1] Hippolyte Taine (1828–93), French philosopher, one of the positivist philosophers in France in the nineteenth century who was interested in making psychology an empirical study. See Taine *De L'Intelligence* (1870), Vol. I, p. 124: 'L'esprit agissant est un polypier d'images mutuellement dépendantes.' (The mind when active is a mass of images which depend one on the other.) Trans. T. D. Haye (Holt & Williams, New York 1872).

Stuart Mill: 'The laws of the association of ideas are to psychology what the laws of gravitation are to astronomy.'[1]

Hume: 1. 'All our distinct perceptions are distinct existences.'
  2. 'The mind never perceives any real connection among distinct existences.'[2]

So the connections are contingent, and are due, not to the nature of the representations, but to chance, to the relationships which these representations have with another in the mind.

This is an attempt to create an autonomous science of psychology (while 'behaviourism' tries to reduce psychology to biology).

What are we to make of this theory?

The well known laws of association are not scientific laws. One idea on its own does not allow us to foresee those that it will call to mind; likewise, one idea on its own does not rule out any other.

For example, the word 'algebra' could be associated for us with the clothes we were wearing the day when we did some problem in algebra, or even with a mark that we had, etc. These laws do not enable us to lay down definite relationships between ideas. We are not told why such and such an idea leads one to make one connection rather than another. To say that representations are independent is to say that they are independent of the mind, of the body, of the object. This is how things would have to be, if we are to think of the life of the mind in terms of psychological atomism.

Criticism of the associationist theory

The main mistake is that those who hold it think of ideas as individual things ('individual' and 'atom' mean the same thing).

Let us try to make a representation of someone to ourselves: one begins with an emotional state. Whenever a representation is produced in the mind thought moves from the abstract to the

[1] John Stuart Mill (1806–73), English philosopher. See 'System of Logic', *Collected Works*, Vols. VII and VIII, ed. J. M. Robson (Routledge & Kegan Paul, London 1973–4).

[2] David Hume (1711–76), Scottish philosopher. See his *Treatise on Human Nature*, ed. Selby-Bigge (Clarendon Press, Oxford 1896), p. 634.

concrete, from what is vague to what is definite, from the general to the particular, from a general impression where all the representations are based on the thought of each representation in succession.

So, the big mistake the associationists made was to think that ideas group themselves together little by little, whereas on the contrary they come about by a process of dissociation.

Unity is a matter of feeling; thought begins from a feeling on which all the representations are based, then it distinguishes between them. We have the same procedure of thought in geometry. All thought always consists in isolating definite things from an aggregate. Thought, in general, is only fruitful when it begins with a feeling. (Cf. Vauvenargues: 'Great thoughts come from the heart.')[1]

Interesting principles of teaching depend on this law of the way thought proceeds: to teach a child to read, one asks the child for a break-down of the words, and not to put the letters together to make up words (word-reading). In the same way, in foreign languages, and in reading obscure authors, it is much better to read it first all at once.

The independent image (which the associationists suppose exists) is an artificial and later product of the mind.

In fact, we perceive the resemblances before the individual things which resemble each other, and, in an aggregate of continuous parts, the whole before the parts. It is not association which comes first; it is through dissociation that we begin.

Summary of criticisms:

1. The so-called laws of association are not laws really because, if we follow them, every representation can bring in its train whatever representation we choose, the choice of one rather than the other remains unexplained.

2. These independent representations are not explained by supposing that they bring others in their train.

3. And, above all, the so-called ideas which are thought of as

---

[1] Vauvenargues (1715–47), French moralist, friend of Voltaire. The quoted maxim is no. 127 in his *Reflexions et maximes*. See *La Bruyere and Vauvenargues*, trans. Elisabeth Lee (Constable, London 1903), p. 171.

psychological atoms which resemble things that exist, have nothing in common with thought; for, in thought, the relationship is already given before the terms that are related; this is so on the intellectual level (the series of numbers is given before the numbers themselves) and on that of feeling (in the case of remembering someone).

From the materialist point of view that we are now putting forward one might say: it is a conditioned reflex, a reproduction of physiological states.

A legend, say, for example, the admiration of some hero or saint, makes us forget that there were times when they acted in an unjust, cowardly or ungodly way. Due to this forgetfulness of ours we invent for ourselves ideas of men which are larger than life, which we force ourselves to imitate.

Love never exists without admiration; one forces the person loved to resemble the image one has of him. It is because this kind of thing happens that feelings have mastery over thoughts. A man who loves someone else will be right because he will see nothing but good in him; if someone else hates the man the other loves he will be right too. One could think of very many kinds of cases in which the attitude of the body dictates to the feelings.

Moral importance of this: what is most important is to try to change the attitude of the body, to break with the associations which drive the spirit from hate to hate, etc. The association of ideas, once it is properly understood, can then be of help in educating others and oneself.

Language

Language is what marks off human beings from everything else. Descartes when he asked himself whether animals think, found an answer to the question thanks to language. If animals were to speak, they would be able to communicate with us. Not even with the best possible training, have horses or dogs been able to speak, though if Europeans go amongst the most savage of peoples, they are able to communicate with them through language. As for animals which have some kind of social structure like bees and ants, there is no reason to believe that they speak. In any case, they have no written language, no written records. They have inherited instincts, but no education.

So, with language, we come to something that belongs to human beings alone.

Kinds of language

A. Spontaneous language: it is something *animal* (and so human too). It is what conveys affections. It is natural in the sense that it is made up of natural reactions of muscles, glands and lungs. It varies from individual to individual.

B. Language proper: it is something that belongs only to human beings. It is what conveys thoughts. It is something artificial in relation to the individual (but natural for society). It is social. Traces of natural language are to be found in it: interjections, onomatopoeia (for imitation is a natural reflex), tone of voice, accent.

But generally speaking, words do not bear any resemblance to things. (One of the delights of poetry is that in it we have a sort of fusion of artificial and natural language.) This feature of language is particularly striking with written language, which is artificial twice over in that the character of the letters do not bear any resemblance to spoken words. If language did resemble things it would lose its value. The relations of words to things are conditioned reflexes: all words can be compared to Pavlov's disc.

With these two characteristics: language is artificial, and language is social, one should be able to explain everything there is to explain about the wonderful power language has.

Language as a means of creating conditioned reflexes

It is through language that every being (for example a dog) undergoes and at the same time brings about (as Pavlov did) a conditioned reflex.

1. Memory: it is on account of language that one can think of such and such a thing. (An example, already mentioned, is that of a prisoner alone in his cell who wants to stop himself forgetting

those dear to him. So he writes their names on the walls of the prison to be sure of creating conditioned reflexes for himself), (one repeats a word, a phrase, one commemorates the dead).

2. Emotions: one can make the conditioned reflex attached to a name so strong that no natural reflex will be able, later, to destroy it. Whenever a lover is in a state which is like that he is in when he is near what he loves, everything seems to him to emanate from what is loved ('crystallisation').

One can help to bring this kind of thing about by words; it is words, names that stay constant for us.

N.B. The more fixed a form of language is, the more suitable is it to express feeling. (Cf. prayers, poems.) One cannot change the lines; the lines of the poem are written in language so formed as to be made unalterable. Due to this, the feeling expressed takes on an unchanging character. For example Lamartine's 'The Lake'[1] has immortalised the regret which lovers feel when they see once more a place where they were in love.

3. Will: this comes into it too because one can will to react in a certain way. Words are fixed, unchangeable as far as we are concerned. (Examples: 'honour', 'integrity', 'theft', etc.) The role of maxims. This is why one uses different words which mean the same thing to bring about different effects. It is a means of influencing oneself, as well as the crowds. Once, after hesitating, one has taken sides in an issue, one repeats the words which present the matter in the light of the side one has taken – just in order to maintain one's position. So words are useful if one wants to act, but full of danger where it is matter of thought, because they egg us on to look at things from a single point of view. Once the word is on one's lips, it can be repeated without end.

4. Attention (a form of will): this is the fourth way in which language is so important in the life of the mind. Once we possess language, there are words amongst those which come to our lips that we can reject: choice of words. For example, when we are doing an exercise in mathematics, we do not write 'sun', but

[1] Lamartine (1790–1869), French poet who entered politics and became Minister of Foreign affairs, but eventually died in poverty. See *Penguin Book of French Verse*, p. xviii and pp. 353 ff.

'triangle', which shows that we are more interested in the problem of geometry than in the sun that shines outside.

Language as having a reality of its own

Language has a reality of its own because it is fixed, permanent, artificial.

It enables us to express ourselves: our tears, cries, groans are states of our own, often brought about unconsciously, but, they are always felt as our own; on the other hand, the word 'pain' has nothing painful about it. As soon as one has given a name to one's feelings one can look on them as objects which have a reality of their own.

Poetry: the wonder of it is that the feeling that is expressed is one's own; the metre adds something artificial in order to compensate for this fusion of artificial and spontaneous language. The poet has a defence against abandoning himself to the feelings he expresses: rhythm, metre, rules.

As for prose, since it lacks these means, any prose work in which feeling is not elevated to the level of thought is weak.

Spoken language: the physiological structure of the ear and the voice can be divided into two parts, one of which acts and the other perceives, and this makes possible 'internal dialogue'. Plato: 'Thought is a dialogue carried on with oneself.'[1] In so far as it is not dialogue, it is no more than reverie, thoughts of the moment. For it to rise above this, for reflection to take place, there must be the two.

Written language is something even more impersonal, especially when it is printed.

Printed prose: (a) it is something external to us, it seems as though it does not belong to us; (b) it has the same appearance for others as for ourselves; in this way it is something that belongs to the whole of humanity.

The more personal a form of expression is, the more implications it has. The more and more objective such means are, the better and better they express what is personal.

It was because Michelangelo went through unbearable conflicts

[1] Plato (427–347 B.C.). See his *Theaetetus*, 189E and *Sophist*, 263E.

with himself that he felt the need to make statues. It was because
Beethoven had felt unbearable joy that he wrote 'The Hymn to
Joy'.

Language is, in short, only one of the arts, prose is one of the
arts; because it is made up of definite signs which produce definite
reflexes it is the art that is best suited for thought.

Language as something easy to handle

Language is something easy to handle because it depends on
movements, it is well defined, fixed, artificial.

We can, thanks to language, call to mind anything we please;
it is language which changes us into people who act.

We are, of course, subject to what exists, but we have power over
almost everything through words. I have no power whatsoever
over the sun and stars; but I have complete control of the word
'sun'. So, 'Open Sesame' is a symbol. Raising the dead, spirits:
words alone call forth the reactions which the thing itself would
call forth. (Cf. Faust, the sorcerer's apprentice, words of good or
bad omen.)

Everything becomes a plaything for us thanks to language.
Through the words I speak, I have the earth, the sun, the stars
at my disposal. No thought would be possible if we were as passive
towards things as we are powerless.

Magic expresses this idea that through spoken words one can
act upon anything whatsoever (an idea which is profoundly true).

Language as a means of coming to grips with the world

1. Through it we possess everything that is absent (it is a support
for memory). We can, of course, have for a moment a general
feeling of something being absent without language; but, apart
from language, we cannot call to mind its characteristics exactly.

Without language, one would never be able to relate what one
sees to what one does not see or to what one has seen. Language
is a bridge crossing over the moments of time. The past, without
language, would only exist as a vague feeling which could not help
us to know anything. Likewise, the future only exists thanks to
language.

2. It gives us order. Thanks to language, the world is like the playthings which children take to pieces and put together again. Order is something which unfolds in time, and depends on a relationship between successive operations. Without language there is no recollection: so, an operation which has taken place would no longer exist.

It is language that enables us to represent the world to ourselves as a small machine (eclipses of the moon using oranges). Language, by allowing us to recreate the world, makes us like the gods, but we only achieve this through symbols. In that case, one sees two ways of thinking of the world.

The two ways in which we come to grips with the world

A. It is language that gives us everything: the past, future, what is far off and near at hand, what is absent and present, what is imagined, the celestial sphere, the atom, etc. but it does this only through symbols.

B. Action (bodily movements) gives us real power, but only on what is present, near to the body's position in space, and is related to needs.

The really important question is to find out whether one has to place all the emphasis on language or all on action, or on both together.

Ethics depends on answering this question.

Must knowledge consist in making principles subordinate to results? (pragmatism). It is one and the same question which has to be answered in the two cases.

We assume that there are two kinds of relationships between ourselves and things: (a) the order resulting from the reaction of speaking; (b) the order which results from acting effectively, but only on that part of the world that is within our grasp at each moment.

Let us compare the relationships which depend on action and those which depend on language.

1. The relationships which depend on action are subordinate to our needs. The sphex, to give an example, only has a relationship with the nerve centre of the caterpillar; if we are running away

from a bull, our only relationship is with the bull's horns. We have no control over what we need; its order is not something ordained: a grain of salt is useless, it is a handful that we can make use of. In the case of a pulley, one needs a weight of more than ten kilograms to lift a weight of ten kilograms. Here, we have a break in continuity in the series of numbers. Hegel: 'Quantity becomes a matter of quality.'[1] Other examples: modern scientific cooking is less healthy than farm cooking.

When one plays the piano, one does not need to know how the strings vibrate.

Needs are always related to wholes; the body is itself a whole which one cannot dissect without making a corpse of it. Needs follow one another by chance. So, it is attention alone that establishes relationships over the order of which we have no control; there is then only an order which is due to chance, so no order at all.

2. What language alone can give us is method, and it can do this for only one reason: because it is so different from what is real. In the world, of course, we have to obey what is necessary. For example, we can carry no more than a certain number of kilos; beyond that all weights are the same for us since we are debarred from them all on the same score (they are too heavy). On the other hand, we can speak of whatever number of kilos we wish, for the word kilo does not weigh a thing. Language enables us to lay down relationships which are completely foreign to our needs.

Take the phases of the moon as an example: we are able, thanks to language, to say that the moon exists even when we do not see it. Words cost nothing, they weigh nothing, we can make use of them to construct an order of things which depends entirely on ourselves.

So let us notice this paradox: it is the order, which depends only on us, that appears as objective, as a necessity.

---

[1] Hegel (1770–1831), German philosopher, of whom Bertrand Russell wrote that 'he is, I should say, the hardest to understand of all the great philosophers'. (*History of Western Philosophy* (G. Allen & Unwin, London 1948), p. 701). See Hegel's *Logic*, trans. William Wallace (Clarendon Press, Oxford 1975), pp. 158–60.

Number is not something that we get from the world; we ourselves, and no one else, are the authors of the series of numbers: for example, the world, in a storm, is not going to provide us with 1 grain, then 2, then 3 grains of sand.

There is no relationship at all between the necessity that $1 + 1 = 2$ and that of feeling the weight of 2 kilos falling on one's head.

So:

(a) Language is the only source of method.

(b) It is language alone that provides us with the necessities which we call objective, in the sense that they are completely independent of our needs, the kind of people we are, our feelings, the situation in which we are placed, etc., etc. The two things go together; without method, no objective necessity. Without objective necessity, no method.

3. All the same, in so far as one rests content with words and nothing else, order and necessity disappear.

Take an example from algebra: there one can add a line to a surface.[1] It is only in language, taken by itself, that one does not need to say '1 pace' before saying '100 paces'. So, the value of language is to be found in a relationship between language and something else. It is action that brings reality with it.

So, we meet a notion we have not come across before: the notion of reality. While action comes after language and depends on it, action itself brings with it something new. There is a difference between saying 100 paces and making 100 paces. It is impossible to deny that there is this 'more' which action possesses in relation to language; or, rather, it is not a 'more', but something quite different: it is reality. One will never, however far one presses

---

[1] This seems to mean that algebra does not determine what it makes sense to add. (I owe this suggestion to Peter Winch.) See also Simone Weil's letter to Alain, probably written in 1933, where she says: 'Descartes never found a way to prevent order from becoming, as soon as it is conceived, a thing instead of an idea. Order becomes a thing, it seems to me, as soon as one treats a series as a reality distinct from the terms which compose it, by expressing it with a symbol; now algebra is just that, and has been since the beginning (since Vieta).' Simone Weil, *Seventy Letters*, trans. R. Rees (Oxford University Press, London 1965), p. 3.

language, come face to face with reality. The question of the reality of the external world becomes then quite a simple one: the simple fact that making 100 paces is something different from saying 100 paces is a proof of its reality.

The unforeseen is what is different from what we find in an ordered language.

One gets the impression that there is some evil power in things when they present us with obstacles that we cannot overcome (landslides). The catastrophes which make us lose our heads, lead us to say: 'Is this a dream?' If, now, one supposes that the same men, faced with the same blocks of stone, instead of reacting blindly, begin to reflect about the situation in an ordered way and use a lever, everything changes: the lever is a means of making a weight less without making the object any less. The stone then loses all its evil character; any weight can be moved by some force; all one needs to do is to establish a relationship between a force of 50 kilos, for example, and a weight of 300 kilos. 'Give me a place to stand, and I will move the world' (Archimedes).

It is this idea that overcomes all the evil force in the world. There is always, between the force at our command and that which opposes us, a relationship such that we will succeed in acting, in leaving our mark on the world, whatever the disproportion between them is. Provided one is able to make this decomposition, the very smallest force can overcome the greatest.

There is a real difference between the man who hurls himself at a stone, who wishes to conquer it through magic, and the man who goes to look for a lever. Notice that it is passion which forces one to take up the first attitude, and that an heroic effort is needed to take up the other. Work continually demands an effort of this kind.

When one hurls oneself against a stone, one feels one is in the middle of a nightmare; but a dream has nothing in common with an action that is governed by an ordered language. But, in what we are now saying in speaking of a stone, etc., there is nothing real because there is nothing unforeseen. In science, in reasoning, one sees in the problems one is dealing with only what one has put there oneself (hypotheses). If in actions there was nothing except what we ourselves suppose them to contain, nothing would ever get done, since there would be no snags. All sorts of accidents can occur between the time when I have seen what the problem is and the time when I have acted. Reality is defined by that. It is what is not contained in the problem as such; reality is what method does not allow us to foresee.

Why is it that reality can only appear like this, in a negative sort of way? What marks off the 'self' is method; it has no other source than ourselves: it is when we really employ method that we really begin to exist. As long as one employs method only on symbols, one remains within the limits of a sort of game. In action that has method about it, we ourselves act, since it is we ourselves who found the method: we really act because what is unforeseen presents itself to us.

One can never give a proof of the reality of anything; reality is not something open to proof, it is something established. It is established just because proof is not enough. It is this characteristic of language, at once indispensable and inadequate, which shows the reality of the external world.

Most people hardly ever realise this, because actions which proceed from reasoning are rare. Or to put it more exactly, it is rare that the very same man thinks and puts his thought into action. (On the one hand we have the engineer who does the thinking, and on the other the worker who does the work.)

Kant[1] has defined art as a miraculous harmony between nature and mind.

This is what enables us to understand that a piece of music is not just something which exists in the mind, but that there is, at each moment, something unforeseen about it. Man's greatness only exists in those moments when he is really conscious of reality. It is very sad that every man does not possess this relationship between language and action which brings reality with it.

We have now, at one stroke, solved both a scientific and a moral question: virtue is the relationship there is between an ordered

[1] Immanuel Kant (1724–1804), German philosopher. See his *Critique of Judgement*, trans. J. H. Bernard (Hafner Publishing Co., New York 1951).

language and action. Intellectual virtue consists in using language in an ordered way and in never making it the slave of success.

The influence which society has on the individual through language

1. This influence makes itself felt first of all by the very fact that language exists. Society, it must be said, is not an aggregate of individuals; the individual is something that comes after society, who exists through society; it is society plus something else. The order is: society, individual. The individual only exists through society and society derives its value from the individual.

2. What is more, it is through the particular characteristics of such and such a language that society exerts its influence. For example, Greek and French are analytical languages which are exactly suited to reasoning. In England, one cannot mention one name like Montesquieu, Rousseau etc. but English is a wonderful means of poetic expression. German is a language which lends itself more to systems than analysis (Kant).

3. Then, there are words.

Words have many senses, like:

head	thought (lose one's head) (*perdre la tête*)
(*tête*)	will (to keep one's head) (*tenir tête*)
	command (to be at the head of) (*être à la tête de*)
value	of money (*d'échange*)
(*valeur*)	moral value (*valeur morale*)
	courage of a thoughtful, deliberate nature (*courage réfléchi et voulu*)
property	personal possessons (*ce qu'on possède*)
(*propriété*)	essential characteristics (*caractères essentiels*)
fortune	goods and money (*biens et argent*)
(*fortune*)	chance (*hasard*)
hearth	fire (*feu*)
(*foyer*)	family (*famille*)
	origin of movement (*origine d'un movement*)
	(a hotbed of conspiracy) (*foyer de conspiration*)

world	κόσμος = arrangement, order
(*monde*)	(κόσμος = *arrangement, ordre*)
	universe (*univers*)
	crowd (*foule*)
	ceremonial gatherings (*réunions cérémonieuses*)
grace	a natural harmony in appearance
(*grâce*)	(*harmonie naturelle dans l'attitude*)
	to grant pardon (*faire grâce*)
	to show gratitude (*rendre grâces*)
	divine grace (*grâce divine*)
sight	the sense of sight (*sens de la vue*)
(*vue*)	a view (*paysage*)
	attitude of mind, etc. etc.
	(*vue de l'esprit, etc. etc.*)

So, language itself already contains thoughts.

It is a natural creation of society; it would be impossible for us to invent a word just like that. (When something new is discovered in science, the words used are quite barbaric, and moreover are derived from Greek or Latin roots, or the scientist's name.)

4. So, due to language, we are steeped in an intellectual environment. It is impossible for us to have thoughts which are not related to all the thoughts bequeathed to us through language. In so far as we give expression to a state we are in, it becomes something that belongs to the experience of all men. So language is for this very reason a means of purification; it is a source of health in the sense that it expresses all the things which torment us. As soon as it is expressed it becomes something general, human, so something that we can overcome.

Aristotle: 'Tragedy is a means of purification.'[1]

Once Goethe[2] had expressed his despair in *Werther* it became a phase through which all people pass.

---

[1] Aristotle (384–322 B.C.), Greek philosopher. See his *Poetics*, trans. I. Bywater (Clarendon Press, Oxford 1940), p. 1449b27.

[2] J. W. Goethe (1749–1832), German poet, dramatist and scientist. His *Sorrows of the Young Werther* (1774) belongs to what is usually called his *Sturm und Drang* (Storm and Stress) period and is a work which Goethe himself later thought little of, and ridiculed.

Any madness in us gains from being expressed, because in this way one gives a human form to what separates us from humanity.

5. Conversely, thanks to language, we are related to someone else's thought as if it were our own. It is impossible to receive a thought without making it our own.

In this way, an exchange of thoughts is made possible. This is what makes up culture; this is why culture is called the 'humanities'. Language creates brotherhood among men. This is very true of written works, but also of popular sayings, myths (the Bible, Greek mythology, fairy-tales, magic), poems, works of art. All these things create community among men, a community not only of thought, but also of feelings. Everyone recognises in Phaedra jealousy, love etc. If, when two men are at loggerheads, the one were to recognise that the other's anger is the same as his own, the quarrel would end.

Language badly used

Language is dangerous in so far as it is something mechanical.

One can put forward a materialist theory of error by thinking of it as language badly used.

We have seen that language is something precious because it allows us to express ourselves; but it is fatal when one allows oneself to be completely led astray by it, because then it prevents one from expressing oneself. Language is the source of the prejudices and haste which Descartes thought of as the sources of error.

One can, if one wishes, reduce the whole art of living to a good use of language.

Reasoning

Leibniz[1] thought that all judgements are analytic for the following reason: the principle of non-contradiction is the fundamental principle, together with the principle of sufficient reason. 'Does anything ever happen without there being a cause or at least a

[1] G. W. Leibniz (1646–1716), German philosopher; the quotation states his principle of sufficient reason. See his *Monadology*, sections 31–2, trans. G. R. Montgomery (Open Court Publishing Co., LaSalle, Ill. 1902).

definite reason for it; that is to say a reason which can be given
a priori why something should exist rather than not exist and why
it should exist as it does rather than in some completely different
way?'

Kant[1] tried to make a list of the principles which are used in
reasoning. He found:

1. The principle of non-contradiction.

2. The categories:

(a) the category of quantity (unity, plurality, totality)

(b) the category of quality (reality, negation, limitation)

(c) the category of relation (the relation of substance to accident,
of cause to effect, reciprocal action)

(d) the category of modality (possibility, existence, necessity).

Kant thought that there corresponded to these categories *a
priori* principles which are the principles of synthetic judgements.

1. All appearances are extensive magnitudes.

2. In all appearances sensation and what corresponds to it in
the object have an intensive magnitude.

3. (a) General principle: experience is not possible except
through the representation of a necessary relation of perceptions
which determine their temporal relationships; (b) substance continues to exist throughout all changes in phenomena, and its
quantity in nature is neither increased nor decreased (cf. 'Nothing
is lost, nothing is created'); (c) all changes are brought about
according to the law of the relation of cause and effect (for Kant
this relation is a necessary succession in time); (d) all substances,
in so far as they can be perceived as simultaneous in space, are
held together by a universal reciprocal activity.

4. What is in accordance with formal conditions is possible; what
is in accordance with the material conditions of experience is real;
that whose agreement with the real is determined according to the
general conditions of experience is necessary.

Spencer:[2] principles are simply general rules which the species

---

[1] See his *Critique of Pure Reason*, trans. N. Kemp Smith (Macmillan & Co.,
London 1929), pp. 41–296.

[2] Herbert Spencer (1820–1903), English philosopher; see his *First Principles*
(Williams & Norgate, London 1908), Part II, chapter 2.

gains by experience. So, there would be no unchangeable principle.

Some apparent absurdities:

Einstein's theories: the speed of light is infinite. On the other hand, he thinks that light travels at 300,000 kilometres a second.

Another apparent absurdity: it seems quite obvious that big and small are relative. There is another law according to which they are absolute.

Theory of sets: there are twice as many whole numbers as even numbers. Nevertheless, one says that the set of even numbers is equal to the set of whole numbers.

We shall adopt the following classification of forms of reasoning:

The syllogism

Example: Socrates is a man, men are mortal; so, Socrates is mortal.

Any proof of the syllogism would be absurd. The syllogism is, to put it briefly, nothing but a rule of language to avoid contradiction: at bottom, the principle of non-contradiction is a principle of grammar.

In general, all ordinary reasonings, which are immediate and performed without effort are more or less explicit syllogisms.

The rules of the syllogism are studied in formal logic.

Mathematical reasoning

Up to the time of Descartes it was believed that it could be reduced to syllogisms.

Let us examine $\left.\begin{array}{l} A = B \\ A = C \end{array}\right\}$ $B = C$

This is not a matter of defining A by B. In fact, would it have any sense, if one did not count? No, the proposition: 'two quantities equal to a third are equal to each other' is not a syllogism; it is not an analytic judgement. One could base a part of science on the proposition: 'equal quantities are unequal' (the infinitesimal calculus), while one would never give credence to a proposition like: 'white horses are black'.

$$\left.\begin{array}{l} A = B \\ B = C \end{array}\right\} \ A = C$$

is an operation which defines a standard.

The elementary operation of arithmetic gives us order. Language comes in very soon; if one stops, it is difficult, without language, to recall where one is; but for all that there is something else involved besides language. Order consists in always doing the same thing again and again. Numbers could not be applied to things or animals if one did not consider the operation which makes one move from one thing to another (pupils in a class, soldiers, etc.).

There are no numbers in nature.

In geometry, even if we consider the matter as materialists, there is always language and order. The syllogism comes in once the demonstration has been made. How does one make the demonstration? With lines. Still, the lines do not exist in nature. How then can mathematics be used for the construction of machinery, for material things like railways, motor-cars?

Where do lines get this magic power from – these faint marks on paper, on a blackboard? The king of the universe is the triangle, or rather, first of all, the straight line.

Let us look for the general characteristics of straight lines, of geometrical figures. Why would one not use the branches of a cedar tree to do geometry?

We see then that geometrical figures are: (a) manageable, (b) simple.

A straight line is simpler than a curve because one can scan it more easily; a straight line is simpler than a surface because one can scan a straight line but not a surface.

It is a mark of our greatness that we can reduce inaccessible things to things that are simple; it is a sign of our weakness that we cannot do this at once.

Further, these figures are: (c) things that are fixed in nature and (d) symbols, which have no solidity, offer no resistance, have no weight, can be used without any chance of mishap.

So, it is just because these things hardly have any existence and are completely in our power that we can use them to gain dominion over the world. (Cf. language through which everything is at our disposal.)

Straight lines are at once symbols of movement (one scans them) and displaceable things.

One could reconstruct the whole of geometry simply by means of these two sorts of movement.

Intuition, inspiration, comes from the fact that one thinks of geometrical figures as things which one can manipulate, draw, and move from one place to another.

What causes inconvenience is precisely this: intuition of movements can lead to error. But why not make use of match-sticks, for example? One could handle those quite well. No doubt, but simply in drawing the figures one lessens the risk of accidents. Accidents – they are what happen unforeseen; an accident can happen at any time whatsoever.

It is time that upsets all our methods. There is nothing surprising in the fact that people have so much trouble in discovering a method: reality and method are opposed to one another.

What is magic about the blackboard and the chalk (or the paper and pencil) is that the blackboard does away with time.

All the same, we are always subject to some sort of time: we cannot construct a polygon before a triangle. But the time involved in this case is not the time which we were considering just now: time is something which regulates action, but everything that is temporally unforeseen is suppressed.

To count to a hundred, to think about a triangle, that is to move in a closed circle.

We can now define method: there is method whenever we suppress that property of time which leads to accidental things happening, and whenever we preserve that property of time which enables us to order our actions.

Order is just that.

Order is a sign of power in so far as it only preserves the actions themselves by suppressing the material content of actions. This is why one might say that geometry lies at the basis of a science of work.

To sum up: the value of the blackboard is that, by using it, we do away with what is accidental, and that we are then not burdened by time. Besides method, geometry also possesses things that signify movement.

In so far as this is so, imagination plays a part.

One can distinguish between three ways of doing mathematics:

1. Imagination can come before language. When this is so, one says that one has found the solution intuitively.

2. Imagination can be present at the same time as language.

One goes through the problem, step by step, in an ordered way, in one's imagination, instead of having a general impression of the solution. Imagination plays a part in this sense: one imagines a step, and the whole problem, however complicated it may be, is reduced to a series of simple steps.

3. Imagination can be absent.

In this case all that is left is language.

In mathematics, as Descartes realised very well, there is no proper understanding except when there is imagination.[1]

The natural sciences

Observation and experiment

Let us find out what there is in the natural sciences that can be called material.

There is, first of all, nature which has two forms: observation and experiment. We find observation alone only in astronomy; experiment always comes in all the other sciences. Human intervention in experiment always involves the construction of an artificial environment.

A. The material apparatus of observation serves to:

1. measure appearances: chronometer, telescope, compass.

2. get rid of anything which hinders the measurement of the appearance (for example, individual factors: e.g. the speed of the nerve-impulse).

---

[1] It may be that there is a mistake in Anne Reynaud-Guérithault's notes, and that Simone Weil said that 'there is no proper understanding except where there is no imagination'. Some of the things she says further on suggest this.

The material apparatus of observation is the necessary and sufficient condition of observation. When one is making observations, it is even necessary not to come to conclusions; one must stop oneself from thinking in order to be completely sure of getting rid of all imagination. So observation appears to be a purely material act.

B. Experiment: this is a device which enables one to establish a relationship between two successive moments of time. What one has to do, in an experiment, is to make an independent world of a finite space, to exclude the real world from the experiment that is:

1. To construct an airtight environment, to limit the experiment to a definite number of finite factors or, to put it in another way, to set aside the infinite: the infinitely large and the infinitely small. In order to set aside what is infinitely large, it is necessary to abstract from the surrounding environment, and in order to set aside the infinitely small, one has to make an abstraction of parts of the factors of the experiment, and parts of those parts etc. There are things which will escape us in both cases. Physics would be something completely different for a physicist whose height was a millionth of a millimetre.

It would be impossible to carry out an experiment if, for example, in the case of a falling body, one had to know what takes place inside the piece of chalk that one is considering. An experiment is, to put it briefly, something artificial. In fact, one cannot completely succeed in getting rid of what is outside and what is within.

But it looks as if all experiments rest on a fiction. So, we see that experiments, just as much as theories, rest on conventions. An experiment without conventions would be an accident.

Properly speaking the idea of an airtight environment hasn't any sense. What sense shall we give it? One can give it a sense as the final term of a series. Everything happens as if it were possible to limit more and more the influence of what is inside and outside, and to do this by means of more and more accurate instruments. The perfection of the experiment depends on human work. This is important, because otherwise one would have no idea of a series, and further because the experiment is part of human experience. It is this that gives a sense to the word 'negligible' in physics. What is 'negligible' is what belongs to the imperfect nature of the airtight environment. For example, in the case of a calorimeter, the amount of heat absorbed by the accessories is negligible because one can make it smaller by using better instruments.

In fact, in an experiment, one is thinking about two unknowns: an ideal experiment and ideal result and these only have sense because the two series converge at the same time.

For example, Joule's[1] law is never absolutely verified, but one can say it is true if its verification is improved in so far as one uses more accurate instruments.

Experiment, then, is not something which, in the last analysis, is opposed to theory: it rests on the same principle, that of order.

In order to apply an empiricism pure and simple, it would not even be necessary to carry out an experiment.
2. A series: a condition which, in appearance, is less general than the first.

What one has to do is: make one of the factors of the experiment vary according to a simple series, and to find out the series in accordance with which the other factors vary. The generally accepted generalisation (water boils at 100 °C) bears no relationship to saying that a law is true for all numbers when it has been found to be true for 1, 2, 3, 4 etc. This latter operation is an attempt to introduce order into nature. The correspondence to be established between different series calls for much deeper research.

First case: one has already thought of a set of series which one tries to reproduce by an experiment. This operation may be called the verification of a hypothesis.

Second case: a blind experiment: one varies one factor, and notes how the other varies, and then one sees if one can construct a series to cover it. Here we have extrapolation and intrapolation.

In the first case mentioned mathematics is what guides the

[1] James Joule (1818–89), English physicist. Joule's law states that the heat produced in a wire by an electric current is proportional to the product of the resistance of the wire and the square of the current.

experiment; in the second, the mathematics is no more than a language which serves simply to give a summary.

First case: hypothesis before experiment.

Second case: hypothesis after experiment.

Hypotheses

Examples: gravity is a constant force; light is propagated in straight lines or in waves, etc.

Other kinds of hypotheses:

A. Hypotheses formed by a deduction which is purely mathematical.

Examples: theory of the lever, theory of floating bodies, the law governing the distances travelled by bodies subject to gravity.

What is the relationship between hypothesis and experiment?

The general opinion is that a scientist puts forward arguments which he submits to nature for approval: if nature says yes, the argument is correct; if it says no, the argument is false.

But one has to take into account that nature and reasoning are different. In nature, order does not exist. What there is first of all in reasoning, which does not exist in nature, is reasoning itself.

'Nature laughs at the difficulties of integration' (Ampère).[1]

Reasoning and nature are different from one another in two ways: there is in reasoning order which does not exist in nature, and there are in nature data which do not exist in reasoning.

If the equilibrium of a balance did not agree with the theory of the lever, one would say that there is something wrong with it.

These kinds of deductions can never be verified because they are the result of perfectly defined data which never exist in nature; they enable us to produce series in nature (a number of weighings more or less wrong).

If these theories are to have an effective application to nature one has to take into account the measure of the difference between the real data and the theoretical data.

Example: the whole of modern thermodynamics depends

---

[1] André Ampère (1775–1836), French physicist and mathematician, pioneer in the study of electricity.

fundamentally on the study of perfect gases, which do not exist (which verify the laws of Mariotte[1] and Gay-Lussac[2].)

B. Hypotheses formed in analogy with a known phenomenon.

Descartes: 'Since in the comparisons I make use of, I only compare movements to other movements, or figures to other figures, that is to say to things which, on account of their smallness, cannot come under the surveillance of our senses as others do, and which, for all that, do not differ from one another more than a large circle does from a small one, I claim that these are the best possible means the human mind has to arrive at the truth about physical questions, even to the point of saying that when someone affirms something about nature, which cannot be explained by any such comparison, I believe I know how to show by demonstration that it is false.'

Analogy is an identity of relationships.

Generally, one mixes up analogy with resemblance. There is no material resemblance between a stone in water and light, but there is an analogy.

C. Hypotheses which rest on algebraic analogies.

Example: Hertz's[3] hypothesis. He made an analysis of electricity. His experiments gave him formulae analogous to those of light. He concluded from this that light is an electromagnetic phenomenon.

There is something remarkable in this kind of hypothesis: one does not know the nature of electricity. One reduces the particular to the general.

Hypotheses of this third kind are very obscure, while the others are quite clear; they cannot be represented in the imagination (though in the case of the second kind they can and must be) they

---

[1] Edmé Mariotte (1620–84), French physicist. The law named after him states that when the temperature is constant the volume of a gas varies in inverse proportion to its pressure.

[2] Joseph Gay-Lussac (1778–1850), French physicist and chemist. The law named after him relates to the expansion of gases – that all gases expand by equal amounts for equal increments in temperature.

[3] Heinrich Hertz (1857–94), German physicist, discoverer of Hertzian waves and the photo-electric effect. See his *Principles of Mechanics*, trans. P. E. Jones and J. T. Walley (Dover Publications, New York 1956).

are independent of mechanical representation. Henri Poincaré[1] says that there is nothing more useless than the mechanical representation of a phenomenon because once one can make one mechanical representation, one can make any number of them. Lagrange has given a single general formula of all mechanical phenomena.

Henri Poincaré said: either a phenomenon verifies the general formula of Lagrange,[2] and then there are an infinity of mechanical representations, or it does not verify it and then one cannot find any representation of it.

In this third kind of hypothesis, algebra takes the place of human thought.

There is a well established basis of a material kind for each kind of hypothesis.

Auguste Comte's[3] table of different sciences:

Hypotheses	*Sciences*	*Methods*
	Mathematics	Demonstration
Mathematical	Astronomy	Observation
Astronomical	Physics	Experiment
Physical	Chemistry	Classification
		(discontinuity)

(N.B. about chemistry: the matter studied in chemistry makes up the conditions of life. The ancient theory of atoms is based on numbers, the modern theory on chemistry (Avogadro's law[4]).

The instrument which brings about the transition from physics to chemistry is the balance.)

---

[1] Henri Poincaré (1854–1912), French mathematician. See his *Science and Hypothesis* (Dover Publications, New York 1952), *Science and Method* (Nelson, London 1914), *The Value of Science* (Dover Publications, New York 1958).

[2] Lagrange (1736–1813), French mathematician and astronomer, who in his *Analytical Mechanics* (1788) reduced the science of mechanics to a few general formulae, from which could be derived all the equations necessary for the solutions of problems in mechanics.

[3] Auguste Comte (1798–1857), French philosopher, often thought of as the founder of sociology. See *The Positive Philosophy of Auguste Comte*, trans. condensed Harriet Martineau (George Bell, London, 1896).

[4] Avogadro (1776–1856), Italian chemist and physicist. The law named after him states that under the same conditions of temperature and pressure, equal volumes of different gases contain an equal number of molecules.

                         Comparison
Hypotheses in   Biology
  physical chemistry   (All these sciences draw their hypo-
                           theses from earlier sciences and still
                           preserve their original character.)

One can add: the sociology studied by Comte, Marx, and the
Marxists, the French sociological school (Durkheim,[1] Levy-
Bruhl[2]).

In search of mind

1. We have seen that language was a means of splitting man up
into two natures – into an active and a passive being: (a) the
creation of conditioned reflexes in himself; (b) an examination of
his own ideas. So, we find in man a duality, two elements which
are different from one another.

2. We have seen, on the other hand, the notion of series which
gives us the sense of the infinite, of perfection.

   Objections: one can represent what is infinite by means of an
ever increasing progression; one represents perfection by means
of the less imperfect.

   Refutation: the materialists say: it is by means of a series of
straight lines more or less perfect than one imagines the perfect
straight line as an ideal limit. That is right, but the progression
in itself necessarily contains what is infinite; it is in relation to the
perfect straight line that one can say that such and such a straight
line is less twisted than some other – and without this the series
would not have any sense. We have here a very good standard for
distinguishing between thoughts which are conceived by the
imagination and thoughts conceived by the understanding. (Cf.
Descartes, Second Meditation: the piece of wax.) There is a complete break between thought and what is not thought, because,
either one conceives the infinite or one does not conceive it at all.

[1] Emile Durkheim (1858–1917), French sociologist, one of whose main
   ideas was that moral ideas can be explained in terms of 'social phenomena' (see p. 203, note 1).
[2] Lucien Levy-Bruhl (1857–1939), French sociologist. See his *Primitive
   Mentality*, trans. Lilian A. Clare (G. Allen & Unwin, London 1923).

3. We have, at last, caught sight of: necessity. There is a fundamental difference between contingent thoughts and thoughts which bear the mark of necessity.

Contingent thoughts: water boils at 100 °C; bodies fall; the sun rises every morning; the continued existence of things we don't see (human beings).

Thoughts which bear the mark of necessity: what is before cannot be after, etc. (Space and time are, according to Kant, the two sources, and the only sources, of synthetic judgements *a priori*.)

Let us examine the notion of necessity more closely.

Necessity only comes into view when thought comes up against an obstacle.

Examples: (a) One loses the notion of necessity when one anxiously looks for something one must find; but when one searches in an ordered way, it becomes obvious by necessity that the thing will not be found in the place one is looking; that one will find it in that place only if it is there.

(b) In a factory people feel giddy, while the trained workman has the idea of necessity because he knows that he can alter the way the machines work.

(c) With regard to passions: Phaedra can have no idea of necessity, because she does not even know what she wants to avoid. It is when the mind is at work that necessity shows itself. In order to understand something necessary the mind must reconstruct it.

The mind makes a tool of the matter which would crush it. It is in so far as man controls nature, whether he does this really, or whether he does it by the use of signs, that he has the notion of necessity.

For there to be necessity there must be encounter, there must be two elements: the world and man (mind). So, materialism destroys itself when it comes up against the notion of necessity.

All human progress consists in changing constraint into an obstacle.

Why must man then run away from the world in order to rediscover himself, face to face, in mathematics? Because the world does not allow him any respite; it is impossible to create a series as long as one is grappling with the real world.

Man is king as long as he is handling his symbols, whereas he is completely powerless before nature. Man cannot construct by placing his hand directly on the world: he can return to the world once he has an abstract construction.

Unfortunately, it is different people who make abstract constructions and who make constructions in the world.

Kant: 'The dove, when in its free flight it strikes the air and feels resistance, might well believe that it would fly better in a void.' (The dove – that is thought; air – that is the world.)

Bacon:[1] 'Homo naturae non nisi parendo imperat.' (Man has command over nature only by obeying it.)

It is only those actions and thoughts which have a necessity about them that are truly human. Whenever one does not have to act, one must avoid those actions and thoughts which have no necessity about them. A thought without necessity is a prejudice. But one has to distinguish between those prejudices which we can do without and those which we cannot do without.

---

[1] Francis Bacon, English philosopher who looked forward optimistically to continuous progress as the result of the application of scientific ideas. See his *Novum Organum, Aphorisms Concerning the Interpretation of Nature and the Kingdom of Man*, no. 3; and Kant, *Critique of Pure Reason*, p. 42.

After the discovery of mind

'No one without geometry admitted.'
(Plato)

Mind: its characteristics

It is impossible to study the mind in a direct way because its characteristics are negative ones.

1. Its duality does not involve two existent things. We can never lay hold of what it is in us that isolates our own thoughts and makes judgements about them.

2. Perfection, infinity.

The first thing that we know about ourselves is our imperfection.

This is what Descartes meant when he said: 'I know God before I know myself.'

The only mark of God in us is that we feel that we are not God. We feel that we should not be imperfect and limited; if it were perfectly right and proper to be so, then we would not think ourselves imperfect; we feel that this imperfection is alien to us.

3. Necessity points to mind well enough, but what we grasp is the necessity of things. There would be no necessity if the mind did not bring it to the surface. The world appears as an obstacle to the mind.

So, if we ever think that we have got hold of mind, it is an illusion.

The study of the mind is not a study which can appeal to any kind of introspection, and *a fortiori*, to observation.

The study of mind can only proceed by looking beyond the thoughts that we express for signs of doubt, perfection, order (necessity). So one can say that the study of mind is related to metaphysics.

Consciousness – unconsciousness.

Degree of consciousness.

Classical philosophy did not raise the question because it admitted only conscious thoughts. In this classical philosophy there was no idea of an unconscious psychological life. Today there is talk only of the unconscious. Leibniz introduced this notion in the following way: he remarked that when one is occupied with something and a very faint noise occurs one does not hear it (a drip of water); nevertheless, one hears the sound of rain (a great number of drops). Leibniz came to the following conclusion: a conscious perception is made up of a number of unconscious perceptions. This is the theory of minute perceptions.

Leibniz also believed it is possible to perceive unconscious thoughts, not only unconscious perceptions. 'Music is a mathematics of the soul which counts without knowing it counts.' Once this notion was introduced into philosophy it was of great importance in the nineteenth century.

General importance of the question

From now on, we have stopped thinking of ourselves as only coming to grips with the material world, as masters of our own souls. We have an idea of a second soul of which we are not masters. One can, in a sketchy way, say that this second soul is thought of in two ways. It can be thought of as the better part of us or as the worse.

The first view is that of Bergson.

The second is that of Freud. For him the subconscious is the place where one represses all the thoughts which should not be allowed to see the light of day because they are bad. Thought, for Freud, is a choice made from among all the psychological phenomena and they are controlled by conformity to social rules.

For Bergson, it is the world and the demands of practical life that exercise this control.

These two conceptions are alike in the sense that they both make appeal to something outside ourselves.

We are going to investigate whether 'psychological phenomena' and 'conscious phenomena' are the same: we shall examine the way in which the notion of the unconscious, of the subconscious, once it is formed, is used and shall try to form a judgement about it. Examples:

Scarcely conscious psychological phenomena: a dull ache which turns out to be toothache; a vague feeling of distress (for example in waking up) which is found to be a memory of some misfortune or other; a vague resentment, etc., some vague feeling of affection about nothing in particular.

Phenomena which are on the verge of consciousness: a continuous noise – one believes one does not hear it, but if it stops, one notices it, so one is conscious without knowing it. Similarly, everything one perceives when one goes to sleep and when one wakes up; every psychological phenomenon which goes with a concentrated act of attention: 'distraction' (something which one did not notice, but which one later remembers); everything which goes with a state of lack of attention (reverie, so well described by Rousseau). There are people who never get beyond such states: children.

On the other hand, when one is attentive, one's consciousness is open to illumination: for example, when one is doing a problem in geometry, if one applies oneself to it; for one may be tired and think about it almost dreamily, unconsciously. Men of genius, one thinks, are those who have unconsciousnesses of genius.

Freud and the subconscious

Examples of the subconscious:

In literature: Hermione,[1] who, subconsciously, loves Pyrrhus and hates Orestes ('Who told you to?'); in *Phaedra*; in the comedies of Molière[2] (*The spite of lovers*). Praise of a man in a high

---

[1] Hermione, a character in Racine's play *Andromaque*. She is the daughter of Menelaus and Helen, and is first the wife of Pyrrhus and then of Orestes. Her jealousy brings about Pyrrhus's death and Orestes's madness. The play was first produced in 1667. See act v, scene iv, l. 1543.

[2] Molière (1622–73), French writer of comedy. See *The Love-Tiff*, trans. F. Spencer (Basil Blackwell, Oxford) and the *Bourgeois gentilhomme*, trans. T. Watt (Nelson Playbooks, London and Edinburgh 1930).

position whom one admires supposedly for his own worth. The way one criticises someone when one says: 'It is not because I feel an aversion to him, but because he has such and such a fault', etc.

(Comedy for the most part is an unveiling of such secret motives.)

The case of the *Bourgeois gentilhomme*: Monsieur Jourdain who thinks he wants to become a cultured person, really wants to show off. Generally speaking, all actions which have vile motives appear to consciousness as having quite different ones.

Every time there is a conflict between what we are and what we want to be, we act so as to appear to be what we want to be.

Freud derived the idea of repression from this simple notion. Everything that we have repressed comes out again in everyday life in the form of dreams and unsuccessful actions and pathologically in the form of neuroses and obsessions. Examples: clumsiness which makes it impossible to do a boring piece of work; missed trains when, really, one doesn't want to catch them, etc.

So according to Freud, unsuccessful acts have their origin in some disturbing tendency.

He studied dreams: they are satisfactions of unsatisfied tedencies, and in particular they are symbolic satisfactions of repressed tendencies or symbolic expressions of repressed thoughts. But, in the dream itself, there is a censor; and for this reason they are only symbolic things. He made a special study of neuroses (the young girl stricken by anxiety at the thought of staying at home alone: she wanted to stop her mother from going to see the person whom she wished to marry). For Freud all neuroses, to put it generally, come from repressed tendencies which are satisfied symbolically. In order to heal these illnesses, Freud thought that it is necessary to find out the subconscious (repressed) tendencies by psychoanalysis (an exhaustive questioning). Then one sees if these tendencies, once brought to the light of day, can be destroyed. He thinks that repression comes from 'taboos', from social prejudices. Now, those things which come most under the influence of society, all have to do with sex.

The consequences of his theories are very far reaching. One has an inkling of their overall intellectual and moral significance: there would be in our minds thoughts which we do not think, in our souls wishes which we do not wish, etc. Realising this would result in freeing oneself from all obstacles.

Freud goes a little way to correcting the demoralising consequences of his teaching by a notion which is nevertheless quite vague: sublimation. There is no doubt that for some people love is a violent desire (Phaedra), for others a work of art (Dante), but that is not clearly explained. This is a correction from a moral point of view, not a theoretical one.

Point to examine: are there really in our souls thoughts which escape us?

We shall make a closer study of this.

Degrees of consciousness

1. A state of reverie, and other cases where one is in a very obscure state of mind (being half-asleep, very tired, certain illnesses).

Rousseau has analysed these very well.

In this state we can distinguish almost nothing; they do not, generally speaking, last for long.

One might say that what is obscure is the object of consciousness and not one's attention. The psychological state is obscure, the consciousness that one has of it is very clear. But why are these psychological states obscure? Because they are passive, emotional states. One is conscious of their passive nature.

The term 'half-conscious', if one uses it, only obscures the question.

2. Absent-mindedness: what is surprising about this state is that thoughts which one is not in the act of forming are present in the mind; there seems to be something paradoxical about this. On this point one does not have to think that there are thoughts which no one thinks, because there is the body. The part of the body on which the mind acts, the action of the mind on the body, this alone is something clear; nevertheless the whole body is in some confused way present to the mind. We are vaguely conscious of bodily mechanisms, not of thoughts.

Unconsciousness

1. Let us take up Leibniz's example again (the minute perceptions). The mind remains insensible to the sound of a drop of water which does nothing to interrput the body's equilibrium. That is nothing surprising, and has nothing to do with consciousness.

2. Attention is often unconscious: when one gives all one's attention to something one is not aware that one is doing it. Descartes: 'It is one thing to be conscious, quite another to be conscious that one is.'

Complete attention is like unconsciousness.

3. Unconscious memory according to Bergson: one can explain it by a conditioned reflex. For Bergson, the mind is a store of unconscious memories which the body draws out of it. (Those become conscious which are in harmony with the state of the body.)

One might just as well suppose that the body is a store of unconscious memories.

4. With regard to what is called 'the association of ideas' there are no ideas; this can be explained quite well by reference to the body.

5. Habit: whatever habit we think of we find they are completely determined by physiological mechanisms. Is there anything else involved? It is true that a mechanical act is very different from something done through habit.

One often says: 'I acted mechanically', in the case of unsuccessful actions and 'That's what I am in the habit of doing' in the case of things one knows how to do. So things done out of habit (one's job) are directed actions; it looks as if there is some unconscious knowledge in habit. This is a difficult question to which we shall return.

Let us point out that one does not need to refer to unconscious knowledge to explain this. Habitual actions which are not mechanical always demand control. (Example: crossing the streets in Paris, playing some game with ease, etc.)

Once something has become a habit, one has always to allow the body to adapt itself to the situation in which it finds itself, but control must always be exercised; only, moments of attention are immediately forgotten, when there is no correction to be made.

One is conscious of the control that one has only when 'things go astray'. No one knows what he is doing when he acts correctly, but, when he makes a mistake, he is always conscious of that. One can compare it to a continual noise one is not aware of; when it stops, one notices it; very much the same kind of thing takes place in the mechanism of the body. So, in something done 'from habit' consciousness can exercise its control in flashes, but one forgets that one has exercised this control. This attempt at an explanation may seem muddled, but it has the merit of trying to give an explanation, whereas the unconscious explains nothing.

The subconscious

The question of the subconscious only really arises in relation to what Freud calls repressed thoughts. It is the most interesting point at issue here. We have to find out whether, in this case too, one can find another explanation of repression, without supposing that there is a container in our soul where we put our well-known bogies.

The phenomenon that Freud mentions has been observed at all times. The devil, in the Christian tradition, which leads one into temptation, can be thought of as the subconscious. Likewise, think of the 'I know not what' in seventeenth-century literature or of *The Spite of Lovers*.

It is certain that we often act from different motives, but that does not mean that we are not aware of these motives.

It often happens that we feel that we are going to think of something; then there is some reaction which stops this thought from taking place. A whole lot of actions would become impossible in actual life if we did not have the ability not to dwell on our thoughts in this way. Examples: in the case of a position gained through foul play, say that of gaining first place through cribbing, one ends up by being proud not only in front of others, but also by being proud with regard to oneself. A man who lives on financial speculation will not allow its true nature to enter his mind – for it is, in brief, theft.

The question is one of finding out how this self-deception works. Are there two kinds of people: one who sets about intriguing to gain the Legion of Honour, and the other who takes it seriously? etc.

It seems that one could do away with the term 'subconscious' as used by Freud, and retain the term 'repression'. It may be that repressed thoughts come out again in dreams, etc. We can say that thought is essentially conscious, but that one can always prevent oneself from formulating it completely. There is a confusion in such ideas because one does not want to make them clear, but, in the case of the subconscious, the consciousness which one has of these thoughts is not obscure. Repression consists in calling something by another name: for example the ambitious man will call his ambition 'public good'. When Hermione explains to Orestes that she hates Pyrrhus, this love of hers for Pyrrhus is not subconscious, it is repressed on account of language. Phaedra thinks that she is going to implore Hyppolytus through love of his son; the repressed desire gets expressed unawares.

There would be no repression if there were no consciousness. Repression is a bad conscience; there will come a time when one no longer needs to repress it.

So, repression is the ability one has for self-deceit. It depends on the duality there is in human nature. But there is no need to say, as Freud does, that one is in no way responsible for the things one represses. One has every right to reproach someone for his subconscious thoughts; one has the right, and even the duty, to do so in one's own case; one has a duty to control them.

Moral importance (the 'choice')

So we have to choose between: believing in a clear conscience, or only believing in degrees of consciousness.

The theories about the subconscious and the unconscious make of us wooden horses in which, following Plato's comparison, there are warriors (thoughts) which live an independent life.

At the other end of the scale, we have Kant's idea: 'I think'.

What one calls the subconscious is something formulated; what is unformulated is what cannot be formulated because it contains a contradiction. While Socrates stands for clear thought, Freud shows us purity and impurity as capable of existing together; that is what is dangerous about his theory. But when Freud speaks of tendencies which come out again through dreams and neuroses, he himself says that what is impure in us should come out again. But, the true way of fighting against subconscious ideas is not to repress anything, but to try to make everything clear in the way Socrates did.

What one must do, is to say: 'What are you thinking about? About a murder. Very well, stop thinking about it.' That is not repression.

We have to bring into the light of open day the monsters within us; and not be afraid of looking them straight in the face. The Catholic religion says that there is no need to be afraid of what we can find within ourselves; that we can find all sorts of monsters there.

So we can conclude that we are responsible for our evil as well as our good thoughts.

What part does the 'self' play in repressed thoughts? It brings about in fact the act of repression. The essence of repressed tendencies is lying; the essence of this lying is the repression of which one is aware.

Freud thinks that psychoanalysis is something scientific; he does not see that it is before everything a moral question.

We are completely responsible for the degree of clarity there is in our own thoughts; we do not always make the necessary effort to become fully aware of them, but we always have the ability to become so. All the observations which tend to establish that there are degrees of consciousness can be accepted, but, when they are not explained by reference to physiological states, they are explained by reference to the non-activity of voluntary thought.

So, in reality, psychological consciousness and moral consciousness are one and the same. One owes it to oneself to achieve this psychological consciousness. All absence of moral awareness is the result of an absence of psychological awareness. All bad action is an action which implies a repression; every action which does not imply it is good.

Personality

The question arises in two ways:

(1) the self as existing in the present;

(2) the self as existing in time.

The self as existing in the present

There are cases where one has the feeling of being two persons at the same time.

But the first thing to say about this, is that, although one says that one is two, one is nevertheless one, since there is one and only one consciousness.

Kant: A unique 'I' is the subject of all thoughts. Nevertheless, there is a struggle. One might explain it either by dividing the soul itself, or by making a division of soul and body. It is absurd to divide the soul, because there is one single being who says 'I'. If there are more of them, there is one of them which says 'You' to the other and this other is an object for the 'I'. ('You shiver, carcass.'[1]) And this doesn't take place as if it were a discussion between friends. There is no kind of reciprocity between the 'I' and the object. It is a fact that, every time one addresses oneself, it is the higher part of our being that addresses the lower part. In the case of Turenne, it is courage which speaks to fear. It is the 'I' which is us, and not the part addressed. The subject which is us is one by definition. It is then mistaken to represent the soul as if it were a theatre. At each moment, there is one will which meets obstacles, and one will alone. This is what Descartes has shown very well in his *Treatise on the Passions*.[2]

'All those conflicts which one usually thinks of as existing between the lower part of the soul which is called sensitive and the

---

[1] 'You shiver, carcass...' This is what the seventeenth-century French general Turenne (of whom Napoleon said that he was the best general before him) used to say to himself during battle when he could not stop himself shivering. The full reported sentence is: 'You shiver, carcass, but if you knew just where I intend to take you next, you would shiver even more.' See Lavisse, *Histoire de France* (A. Colin, Paris 1912), chapter 14, p. 107.

[2] Descartes, *Treatise on the Passions*, Article 47.

higher part which is called rational, or better between natural
appetites and the will, is nothing but the aversion which exists
between the movements which the body through its animal spirits
and the soul by its will have a tendency to excite at the same
time. For there is in us but one soul alone, and this soul has in
itself no division of parts; it is the same soul which is sensitive and
rational, and all its appetites are voluntary. (notice:
"appetites" = "tendencies"). The mistake which has been made
in making the soul play the part of different persons which are
thought to be opposed one to the others is the result of not
distinguishing clearly its functions from those of the body, to which
alone one should attribute what can be noticed in us which is
opposed to our reason.'

In the first instance we take into account what the body tells
us; then there is a second stage when we separate it off from
ourselves.

Identity in time

One connects what one was to what one is by a succession of
necessities; but, since one cannot think of oneself as an object, one
has to represent yesterday's self to oneself in analogy with that
of today. Amnesia does not result in one's losing consciousness
of the 'I'. One can lose consciousness of oneself in so far as one
is an object, but not in so far as one is a subject.

One can distinguish between three kinds of consciousness of
oneself.

1. Consciousness of oneself as a subject: at such moments one
fills the world. (Cf. Rousseau after an accident: 'At that moment
I was being born.')

2. Consciousness of oneself as an object: one knows that one has
a name, a position in society, etc.

3. Consciousness of oneself which is a combination of the two
previous kinds: that is the normal state.

Abnormal states are those in which one is conscious of oneself
only in the first or second way.

In the first case one loses consciousness of the limits of one's
power; that is why this is a delightful feeling (see Rousseau).

In the second case, one looks at life without taking any more interest in oneself than in some object. The question of personal identity properly arises in so far as we have consciousness of ourselves as subject and object at the same time.

We remember our past states only in so far as they were active. Everything we passively undergo we forget, and we remember it only in so far as what we undergo is an obstacle to our acting.

To sum up, any facts that we can mention about conflicts of personality, any internal struggle, any alteration in memory, does not affect our internal unity.

We have a number of ways of remembering ourselves as objects: our name, our social rank, our jobs, our dress, other people's attitudes towards us, etc. Society reminds us all the time that we are 'so and so' and not someone else. That is why our memory of ourselves is stronger than that of anything else.

There is something else too: we are ourselves the seat of our own conditioned reflexes.

The desire to escape from oneself as an object results from romantic feelings, and everyone feels this some time or other.

Judgement

The distinctions which logicians make

Logicians distinguish between concept, judgement, reasoning.

1. Concept: this is the kind of term from which one can construct judgements or arguments. In a syllogism there are three concepts. The verbs, apart from the verb 'to be', the substantives, are concepts. (N.B. Existence is something different from ordinary concepts. Existence adds nothing to the concept of a thing.)

2. Judgement: this is a relationship between concepts.

3. Reasoning: this is a relationship between judgements.

The question's significance

What is of interest here is to find out what a judgement is in so far as it is an operation of the mind. It is in essence a relationship. One can then think of judgements made in action, without words (choice). Kant distinguished between: analytic judgements and synthetic judgements. But analytic judgements are not judge-ents; they do not go further than the concept. (N.B. There are cases where one repeats the same word and where nevertheless the judgement does go further than the simple concept itself. For example, when one says: 'A child is a child' or: 'Duty is duty'. These judgements are, in fact, synthetic ones, for the same word has a different sense.)

Judgement is an activity of the mind. The real bond in all judgements is the 'I'.

Kant: 'All relations are acts of the understanding', that is to say: no relationship is given as it is, they are all works of the mind. This is very important; it forbids one from believing that relationships come to the mind from outside, that is to say that in no case is knowledge a simple reflection of things. Matter is completely devoid of relationship, it is thought that is relationship. We never know things as they are in themselves, because that would involve never beginning to think (that is why one looks to what is completely alien to reason as the source of oracles: the Pythia).

The ideas of reason cannot resemble the world. Kant: 'We cannot represent to ourselves any kind of relationship as existing in the object without having first made the relationship ourselves.'

Judgement is the essential faculty of the mind. It is high praise to say of someone: 'He is a man of judgement.' Kant called this faculty of making relationships 'the original synthetic unity of apperception'.

One might say that all thought is judgement. There is no scientific thought nor experience apart from judgement. 'Experience is knowledge which comes from related perceptions.' The most commonplace experience is impossible unless the mind makes this kind of relationship.

Different theories of judgement

1. There is the associationist theory, according to which 'judgement is an association of ideas'.

This theory is confused with that of Condillac (who came before the associationists).

This theory is absurd, because judgement is either an affirmation or a negation.

2. The materialist theory: it rests on the experiment with the monkey choosing boxes.

But one can say that there is a difference between action which implies a comparison, and the mind which grasps the comparison on its own account.

Man, in so far as he is mind, does not accept the illusions of the sense.

3. The fideist theory (N.B. fideism is the view that any affirmation of the mind does not come from reason, but from feeling): one believes something because one wants to believe it; belief in certain things becomes an obligation. Fideism is a view very well suited to all forms of spiritual tyranny; fideism always ends up in the subordination of thought to a social myth.

But the fact that doubt is possible shows that fideism is false. What is more, whenever one tries to suppress doubt, there is tyranny.

Fideism confuses 'judgement' and 'belief'. In fact, they are confused whenever one does not try to distinguish between them. One can only distinguish between them through doubt.

4. Descartes' view (cf. Fourth Meditation, on error): Descartes distinguished between the faculty of conceiving relationships (understanding) and the faculty of affirming relationships (judgement). The faculty of affirming is unlimited or absolute; on the other hand, the faculty of conceiving is limited and a matter of degrees. Judgement is something whose value consists in the fact that it can be suspended (doubt). (This idea of Descartes' has been taken up by Rousseau in a passage where he shows that judgement is something active.)

According to Descartes, the mind can conceive a relationship without affirming it, because it can doubt.

(N.B. Judgement, one could say, is exercised too in the case of reasoning. So one has to understand 'judgement' in a wide sense, like Descartes.)

Descartes, Rousseau and Kant had a similar view of judgement.

5. Rousseau's view:[1] 'I reflect on the objects of my sensations, and,

---

[1] Jean-Jacques Rousseau (1712–78), French philosopher. See his *Emile*, trans. Barbara Foxley (Everyman Library), pp. 232–3. There is one

finding that I have in myself the faculty of comparing them, I feel endowed with an active power which I did not know I had before. To see, that is to perceive. To compare, that is to judge. To judge and to feel are not the same. Through sensation, objects are presented to me in isolation, as separate, as they are in nature. In comparing them, I change their position. I transport them, so to say, I place them one upon another in order to pronounce upon their difference and their similarity, and in a word, on all their relationships...

'I search in vain among my senses for this intelligent power which intervenes and then makes a pronouncement. For they are passive in nature and perceive each object separately or at least they will be able to perceive a complete object made up of two (as the monkey did) but, not having any ability to place them one on the other, they will never compare them, and will make no judgement about them.' (The monkey does not construct a whole out of them, its experience of them is purely passive.) 'When someone asks me for the cause which determines my will, I ask in turn what is the cause which determines my judgement, for it is clear that these two causes are just one, and if one has a proper understanding of the fact that a man is active in the judgements that he makes, and that his understanding is only the power of comparing and judging, one will see that his freedom is only a similar force or derived from that; he chooses the good in so far as he has judged what is true; if he makes a false judgement, his choice is bad. What then is the cause which determines his will? It is his judgement; and what is the cause that determines his judgement? It is his faculty of intelligence, his power of judging; the cause which brings this about exists in himself.'

(One can see how much Kant was influenced by Rousseau.)
6. Spinoza's view:[1] it is a polemic against Descartes.

According to him, every idea implies an affirmation; activity is contained in the ideas, not in the mind. 'Ideas are not dumb

sentence missing in the passage quoted. It is: 'On my view the distinctive faculty of an active and intelligent being is the ability to give sense to the word "is".'

[1] Spinoza, *On the Correction of the Understanding*, pp. 234–63.

pictures.' All ideas are affirmed as being true; the only thing that makes one think that an idea is false is another idea which comes to oppose it. Cartesian doubt is declared to be impossible by Spinoza. One suspends one's judgement, Spinoza says, when one has reasons for doing so, not by an arbitrary decision. Spinoza denies liberty. He thinks of God as being the aggregate of all things. It is never man thinks, it is God who thinks in him. So vice, like error, is something inadequate; it is an action whose principles are inadequate ideas.

Spinoza's view of the matter results in doing away with man, while Descartes', on the contrary, thinks that man is God's equal through his faculty of judging and affirming.

To sum up, four views of judgement (those of the associationists, the materialists, the fideists, Spinoza's) result in the denial of judgement.

One has to choose: the only real choice open to us as honest people is the theory of Descartes and Rousseau.

Reasoning
Analytic and synthetic

One distinguishes between: analytic reasoning and synthetic reasoning.

Analytic reasoning is of no interest. The syllogism is an example of it. It works by substitution (it is well known that one cannot substitute subject for predicate or inversely).

In the Middle Ages, this kind of reasoning was common practice. What is more there was at that time no theoretical progress in thought.

Synthetic reasoning: that is a construction. It includes: deduction, induction, reasoning by analogy. One might add: the elaboration of hypotheses. Let us first of all take a brief glance at these forms of reasoning and then we shall make a more detailed analysis of them.

Deductions are synthetic *a priori* reasonings which all depend on space and time (Kant): they depend always on time and sometimes on space.

Induction can be thought of as an application of the principle:

'Relationships which recur often can be thought of as constant.' In induction, there is a purely mechanical factor, habit, but one also assumes that this constant character of events is a sign of necessity. Since this necessity is something that we have assumed to exist, and have not established that it does exist, we have recourse to an elaboration of hypotheses.

Reasoning by hypothesis

'If one assumes that...then the result is that...'

In passing from an hypothesis to its consequences one works by deduction.

Reasoning by analogy

Example of a watch: when one has taken one to pieces, one thinks that all the others work in the same way.

Reasoning by analogy is not rigorous, but it is indispensable, because we cannot take everything to bits.

N.B. analogy is not at all the same thing as resemblance. In its proper sense, 'analogy' is a mathematical relationship, a proportion. In the case of a watch, one thinks that there is the same relationship between the way one watch looks and its movements and the way another one looks and the way it works.

There are cases where the identity is not complete.

There is a continuous link between all the forms of reasoning: if there is no hypothesis, induction does not exist except as a matter of habit; hypothesis presupposes deduction and analogy.

We shall make an analysis of these different kinds of reasoning and see where they apply (that they are involved in ordinary thinking is not the currently accepted view).

Deduction

Deduction is synthetic. It is an invention. There is something paradoxical about deduction; it does not consist simply of given facts and it is inexhaustible. There is always something new in mathematics.

Deduction is *a priori* and there are different theories about its *a priori* nature:

Plato's[1] theory is based on 'reminiscence': we have known everything, but we have forgotten it all; the proof that we have lived in another world is that we make inventions in mathematics. Plato explains by the idea of forgetfulness the things one knows and what one does not know.

Descartes' theory: is that of innate ideas. Descartes would say that some ideas are the work of the mind. But those inferior followers of Descartes and those who seek to refute him are mistaken; they believed that Descartes meant that *a priori* ideas are born with us.

Kant's theory (N.B. It is due to him that the term *a priori* is used.): the difficulty arises just because of the absurdity of the theory of innate ideas; these ideas do not exist outside of ourselves, but within us; but, in that case, how do we have so much trouble in discovering them?

What is *a priori*, is what we do, it is what comes from the activity of the mind; what is *a posteriori* is what the mind passively receives. By form Kant meant what is *a priori*, and by matter what is *a posteriori*. The two are inseparable.

In ordinary experience, what is *a posteriori* is an occasion for, or an object of, thought; in *a priori* reasoning what is *a posteriori* are symbols, images.

The relations of cause and effect is *a priori*, particular causes and effects are *a posteriori*. What is *a priori* is an act of understanding. The idea of a relationship between one thing and another can be misapplied, but it is always true.

One can say then: we supposed that we found within ourselves what is *a priori*; but the subject can draw nothing out of himself, he has to construct; if ideas could be drawn out of ourselves, they would be things. So it is not surprising that we have to make an effort.

[1] Plato's theory of 'reminiscence' is put forward in his *Phaedo*.

Space and time

According to Kant it is space and time that bring about the relation between form and matter: space and time are '*a priori* forms of sensibility'.

Space

1. One sometimes thinks of it as something empirical: that is the genetic theory of space (that is to say that the idea of space is something which is developed). This theory depends on two ideas.

(a) Visual stimuli, according to Spencer:[1] when one has a series of visual sensations, the fact that each continues gives the impression that the sensations are simultaneous; and Spencer thinks that when one has the notion of simultaneity one has the idea of space.

(b) The idea of two temporal series, inverse to one another, makes one think that the causes of sensations which succeed one another are simultaneous.

Criticism of this theory:

(a) 'Simultaneity' is not the same thing as 'space': I can hear sounds, I can think of something at the same time as I see without giving my thoughts any position in space.

(b) Spencer's view is inadequate because he has not seen the idea of necessity that there is in space. (Comparison between the succesion of the ascending and descending scale and the succession of lines made up by the floorboards which one can walk over. I cannot take the third step before I have taken the second, while I can sing the 'me' before the 'doh'.)

It is the idea of space which gives the idea of reversibility, and not the other way around.

There is another (German) form of the genetic theory (Wundt[2]): one gives a position to sensations because each point of the body gives a different sensation; these purely qualitative sensations are changed into data which can be thought of as extended.

[1] Spencer *First Principles*, Part II, chapter 3.
[2] Wilhelm Wundt (1832–1920), German philosopher and psychologist; a pioneer in experimental psychology.

Criticism of this theory: Wundt has shown how one can relate some sensation to some point in space, but, before that can happen, one must have the idea of space.

2. The naive theory: the idea of space is given to us with sensations themselves.

(a) Some philosophers have believed that space is given to us through sensations of touch; (b) others have believed it to be due to sensations of sight (Lachelier[1]).

'In fact, it is time which plays the role of space for someone born blind; distance or nearness only have meaning for him in so far as a greater or lesser length of time elapses between one sensation and another.'

Criticism: but if one adopts this theory for someone born blind, one has to do so for ourselves too. We relate our visual sensations in exactly the same way as the blind person relates his sensations of touch; some blind from birth do geometry.

(c) Other philosophers have thought that space is given us both by sensations of sight and by sensations of touch.

(d) William James[2] thought that we get it from all sensations.

Criticism: if space was *a posteriori*, geometry itself would be *a posteriori*.

We conclude that space is *a priori*. But space is different from other things that are *a priori*. There are with regard to space things which we must accept without understanding them (three dimensions). One cannot deduce from the notion of space that space necessarily has three dimensions.

Three-dimensional space is a condition of experience. The idea of an object would not exist without the idea of three dimensional space; it is due to this idea that one can have experiences. One hand will never occupy the space of the other (there is equivalence not identity). There is something here that is given to us; it is a paradox we submit to.

---

[1] Jules Lachelier (1832–1918), French philosopher, who was mainly influenced by Leibniz and Kant, and to whom Bergson dedicated his *Time and Freewill*. See his *Psychologie et metaphysique* (Paris 1949).

[2] William James, *Principles of Psychology*, Vol. II, chapter 20.

Time

This too is an *a priori* idea. (One might say that the idea of time comes from the idea of change, but in order to have the idea of change, one must have the idea of time), and although time is not invented by us, it contains many paradoxes (see plan for essay on 'Time').

The privileged role of space and time:

This is Kant's conclusion. Let us try to think about it.

The idea of time has the superiority.

In so far as we are passive we do not have the idea of space (there must be movement) nor that of time (we are limited to the present moment).

Time is what limits our actions; it is in a way the only sign of our weakness. (One cannot return to the past, nor obtain something at once.)

All limits are given us through time, but we only meet these limits when we are active (reverie, sleep do not have these limits).

Space is the special application of the law of time to our actions.

Space and time are then the form which is set upon all our actions: it is on account of this that space and time are the form of all our synthetic *a priori* judgements.

To conceive the pure laws of time and space is to conceive the obstacles which they put in our way; to try to relate all our actions to time and space is to try to conceive the world, no longer as a dream, but as an obstacle.

Causality

Causality means looking for what is necessarily prior: 'One cannot get to one place before one has got to some other' is the model of necessary successions. One finds necessary successions in natural phenomena whenever one reduces them to motions. One then comes upon the idea of a mechanism.

Descartes: 'Everything is figure and motion.'[1]

To relate things in this way to time and space is to act as if we

---

[1] Descartes, *Principles of Philosophy*, Part IV, Principle 198.

have constructed the world by acting according to a method; we have no other way of explaining nature.

Descartes lays that down as the ideal of science. But we know very well that the world has not been constructed by us nor by a being who is like us. Our action is never that of a creator, it is that of changing one thing into another. Every intelligible explanation is a matter of understanding how one thing changes into another.

For, we know very well that nature could not have been created by changing one thing into another, nor by a limited being, because it is infinite. We act as if a limited being, similar to ourselves, had tried to bring things into existence. Explanations are always related to ourselves.

Another thought: we can only lay down a causal relationship between two points of time separated from one another by some length of time; when we give our explanations of nature, we are in this way making a relationship between separated moments of time; and we know all too well that, in nature, that has no sense.

The value of knowledge

All this is very important. One sees that all our knowledge is hypothetical (in the sense that the celestial sphere is an hypothesis).

Nevertheless, to explain nature is the only way we have of thinking of it as an obstacle to our acting in a methodical way. Science is inadequate, but it is only when we understand this inadequacy that our science has a value. This enables us, in passing, to pass judgement on pragmatism. The pragmatists place 'method' and 'result' on the same level. One might say, with the pragmatists, that all science reduces itself to a process of action on nature, but it is necessary to add the word methodical.

Reality comes into view when we see that nature is not only an obstacle which allows us to act in an ordered way, but it is also an obstacle which infinitely transcends us.

The inadequacy of hypotheses enables us to understand that nature is not a simple concept.

The idea of God as creator of the world: when we try to apply our thought to the world, God the creator is the model of our application of it. If our thought were perfect, we would think that we had made the world. Science would not have a perfect model apart from the idea of God the creator.

Between the man who believes in God and the man who only believes in the human spirit there is no real difference (if one doesn't allow the superstition of miracles to come in: the idea of miracle is an impious one). It is only the materialist view which completely does away with the idea of God.

So, every effort to understand natural phenomena will be an effort to recreate the world through synthetic judgements *a priori* which depend on space and time, that is to say through mathematics.

Kant: 'We only know how things appear to us', because we have not made things and we try to imagine that we have. This is a 'hypothesis', but the hypothesis rests on relations of space and time which do not belong to nature.

Space and time are foreign both to nature and mind, to nature because they imply relationships which only have sense for thought and to mind because there are in these relationships things of which we can give no account.

We do not know things in themselves, but what we know is something different from appearances.

(It would, in any case, be a contradiction if thought could get at things in themselves.) Things as phenomena are different from things as appearances.

A phenomenon is experience with all the necessary relationships that it implies, while there is no necessity in appearances.

One can, then, make the following summary of Kant's analyses of the act of knowledge:

1. No knowledge is possible without sensible experience; it is the world which has to furnish the matter; the mind alone can only provide a form without matter. (Kant: 'The dove when, in its free flight, it beats the air and feels its resistance, might believe that it would fly even better in the void.')

2. No experience is possible without *a priori* judgement.

Everything that we call 'objective' in experience is what appears in it as necessary.

The difference between an objective succession and a subjective one (real or apparent) is brought about by the idea of necessity. Whenever we speak of reality, there is necessity. The idea of the object which is in front of me, is the idea of a necessary relation between all its appearances.

There is no need, as Hume did, to start out from experience and then look for some relation between experiences; one will find nothing but chance.

One has to see that necessity is prior to experience. Necessary connections are the conditions of experiences; they give to it the form without which experience would only be a mass of sensations.

Order

In deduction, the essential role is played by time. Kant saw this very well. Time serves as a schema. The model which we construct when we want to understand something in recreating it is always a certain succession. The role of time in thought consists in this: that the idea of order provides a method for understanding whatever we think about. For, order is inseparable from time.

With order, we pass on to Descartes.

There are simple things which are given to us all at once. The sign of something real in human thought is in fact postulates, etc. The mind cannot think what is contrary, even when there is no contradiction in doing so. Still, God can create the world just by thinking of it.

It is from these simple things that one starts, and it is a question of reducing complex things to simple things. We are forced to accept the postulates and axioms precisely because we are unable to give an account of them. What one can do is to try to explain why they seem obvious to us.

Mathematical invention

A. The reason why there are difficulties in mathematics where one has all the data is because they are not given to us in order. One is sometimes led to look for what is simple starting from what is complex and take in many relationships at once.

When we construct a series for ourselves, the ideas that we have are made up by us. But how are we given the terms of a series which we have not made? That can be provided by life, by what is external to us. Examples: Thales,[1] who was asked to measure the pyramids; problem of the duplication of the cube for the temple of Apollo.[2]

When nature provides us with the data:

1. Invention may proceed by our groping about: that is then called 'intuition'. In fact it is chance. We ought not to admit that 'intuition' is some kind of intelligence; it is a matter of feeling.

2. Invention which has method about it proceeds by analysis and synthesis, (we have the application of Descartes: second and third rules).[3]

In the duplication of the cube, for example, one has first of all to find where the difficulty lies and then follow Descartes: thirteenth rule: 'When we have a complete understanding of what the question is, one has to do away with any superfluous idea, reduce it to its simplest elements, and subdivide it into as many parts as possible.' In the case of the cube, what is the difficulty? It is one of doubling? We know how to double a number, a length. The difficulty begins with a surface. We know only too well how to double the side of a square; but if we do that we make the square four times as big.

We are given the relationships between two squares; one has to reduce it to relationships of lengths. A case where we know how

---

[1] Thales (*c.* 640–*c.* 547 B.C.), who is often thought of as the first of the Greek philosophers, a native of Miletus in Asia Minor. It is reported that he made practical application of the geometry known to him to measure the height of pyramids in Egypt. See John Burnet, *Early Greek Philosophy* (Adam & Charles Black, London 1930), pp. 40 ff.

[2] The duplication of the cube refers to what is sometimes called the Delian problem, the temple of Apollo being on the island of Delos in the Aegean Sea. The problem is to find a method for constructing, with geometrical instruments, an altar which has the shape of a cube and which has a volume which is twice that of a given cubic altar. See Francois Lasserre *The Birth of Mathematics in the Age of Plato* (Hutchinson & Co., London 1964), pp. 114 ff. and Thomas L. Heath *A History of Greek Mathematics* (Clarendon Press, Oxford 1921), Vol. I, pp. 246 ff.

[3] Descartes: 'Rules for the direction of the understanding' in the Haldane and Ross translation.

to double surfaces: a case where it is sufficient to double the lengths (one can double a square on condition that one has no longer a square, but a rectangle). So the question amounts to this: to find a square equal to a given rectangle. The best way to proceed is to suppose the problem solved (that is Descartes' great discovery). Then, one will ask oneself why the duplication of the cube is more difficult than the duplication of a square. In this case too, we proceed by supposing the problem solved. The rectangle and the square are defined by only two sides, here there are three. One will forget completely about cubes; one will state a problem in terms of straight lines.

So, one has to:

(a) isolate the difficulty, eliminate everything in it which is accidental. What is accidental in this case, is the cube. (What holds us up in our thinking, is that we have to think of a series of four proportions according to an order which is contrary to the nature of these relationships.)

(b) find a way of imposing on the mind an order which is opposed to its nature.

How, nevertheless, are we to think rationally? This is the great discovery of algebra, of unknowns (taking the problem as solved). What one has to do is to try to find a series which covers all aspects of the problem.

The first kind of assimilation of an unknown is the method that lazy pupils use when they try to answer a problem by imagining some solution or other by chance, then they look to see if 'it fits'.

The second kind was discovered by Diophantus[1] – *regula falsi*, that is: 'the rule of taking what is not right'. Diophantus started by doing exactly what the lazy pupil does, then he looked to see why 'it does not fit'.

The third kind, is the method of a series: one allows the variables to vary and sees how the function varies; the correct value of the variable is the one that corresponds to a given value of the function. One can assimilate the unknown to a variable.

[1] Diophantus (date uncertain, between 150 B.C. and A.D. 280). He was the first of the Greeks to develop an algebraical notation, and it was his writings which led Fermat to take up his work in the theory of numbers.

One has to succeed in creating series which the problem itself requires one to survey in the reverse order. One has to succeed in surveying these series the right way round thanks to unknowns, to variables.

B. But the problem of invention poses itself in another way: how can the working of the mind lead the mind itself to problems? (up to now the problems have arisen by chance). How can the mind, by methodical research, furnish itself with difficult problems to solve?

This happens whenever a definite method meets its own limit (and this, of course, happens, to a certain extent, by chance).

An example of this is the method the Pythagoreans[1] used. They ran up against the diagonal of the square which exhibited incommensurables.

Why were relations between magnitudes and relations between numbers confused in the first place? The reason for this happening was that two notions contained in the figures were confused: order (a series of numbers) and the division into small parts (6 is divisible into 6 small parts). This second idea is only of use to the imagination. What satisfies the mind is order, and that is not divisible: 5, in so far as it is the fifth term of a series, is not divisible into 5 small bits. When one applies arithmetic to geometry one has to see only order (Eudoxus's[2] method).

There are some cases where one succeeds in solving a difficulty by the idea of a limit.

Then, one comes to questions where one no longer understands what the difficulty is (transcendent numbers: π, e). One has to take

---

[1] The Pythagoreans, pioneers in the study of mathematics amongst the Greeks. One of the first problems they ran up against was that the diagonal of a square could not be expressed as a rational number. The proof of this is to be found in an appendix to Book x of Euclid's *Elements*. The Pythagoreans used the Greek word *logos* to refer to number, and seem to have coined the phrase *logos alogos* (a logos that is not a logos) to refer to the incommensurability of the diagonal of a square, which we now refer to as an irrational number. (Someone might argue that it is no more irrational or *alogos* than any other number.)

[2] Eudoxus (*c.* 406–355 B.C.), Greek mathematician and astronomer, who was a member of Plato's Academy. For his contribution to mathematics and astronomy see François Lasserre, *op. cit.*, pp. 85–168.

refuge in algebra, and then one has reached the stage when signs have become a fetish: 'imaginary numbers'. One doesn't understand why imaginary numbers make calculations easier, and mathematicians do not worry about it. In our days mathematical invention is a matter of making calculations easier.

Deduction as what prepares the way for experiments

It is deduction that provides us with the ideal in making experiments. In fact, in an experiment, one seeks to achieve a controlled environment. Now, in mathematics everything is under perfect control; there is nothing in it except what we have put there ourselves. One brings about one change, another change takes place; one is certain that this second change is the result of the first.

But it isn't enough to say: 'Such and such a cause brings about such and such an effect'; one has to establish a quantitative relationship, to see how much the effect varies. How can one make the effect a function of the cause? One cannot do this without experiment, nor by a single experiment. So, intrapolation? extrapolation? This is induction pure and simple, but it does not satisfy the mind. For it to do so, there must be continuity. So, if there is a controlled environment and continuity, we have nothing but deduction. That is found only in geometry. What prevents physics being like geometry is, in a word, the world! So once again we have not dealt with the nature of experimenting. One can simply say that geometry is a series of perfect, ideal experiments, straining the sense of the word 'experiments'.

Examples: the lever, Archimedes'[1] principle.

The lever allows us to determine whether a balance is accurate or not.

As for the law of Archimedes, one classifies fluids according to the way in which they agree with it. The importance of this law is independent of practical considerations: what one does is to

---

[1] Archimedes (*c.* 287–*c.* 212 B.C.), one of the most gifted of Greek mathematicians who met an untimely death at the hands of Roman soldiers in Syracuse. See Thomas Heath, *The Works of Archimedes* (Cambridge University Press, 1912).

interpret the experiment in an ordered way (defining the viscosity of fluids).

These laws have a theoretical value in so far as they are independent of experience, and a practical value in so far as experience approximates to them.

The value of deduction

Pure deduction: there is one sort whose value is nil: that is the syllogism.

As for deduction proper, it seems, at first sight, that this form of thought is perfect. When one looks more closely at it, one sees that it is in fact imperfect:

1. due to order, which is a hindrance to thought as well as its only support. (Order hinders us, for example, when we try to find proportional means.) Order is for thought a prison all the more real as nature pays no attention to it. The actual problems we have to deal with, therefore, all militate against order.

2. because deduction must use symbols which are both an obstacle and an indispensable aid. (Numbers themselves were an embarrassment to the Pythagoreans.) Each step the mind takes consists in handling symbols. One has to think of the method independently of symbols: it is this which makes for advances in mathematics. Today, on the other hand, people have allowed themselves to become carried away by symbols; they are arrived at the point of getting results which they do not understand.

These two imperfections of deductive reasoning are the two principles which govern invention in mathematics. It is something which has no end, and could not have one. One understands how someone can have a passion for mathematics. To do mathematics – that is to try, unceasingly, to reach out for one's own thought. So the whole of morals is to be found potentially in mathematics; one has to overcome one's tendency to allow oneself to depend on chance, which is the sin of sins, the sin against the Spirit. And there, in mathematics, one is not helped by anything. (In action, one is helped by another action; for example anger helps one to show courage.)

That is why Plato said: 'No one admitted who doesn't know geometry.'

The application of deduction

1. Application of a law.

This has a theoretical value too because, when one thinks that a law is more or less applicable, one inevitably thinks of a relation of cause to effect. Example: Archimedes' law is not perfectly applicable because fluids are not perfect. But the man who, for the first time, made a boat of iron applied the principle of Archimedes, although he knew very well that it was not completely applicable. One is able to think of this floating boat by reference to an actual relationship of cause to effect.

It is very important to be able to think as much as possible of actual causal relationships because that makes action easier for us.

To do science, is to think of oneself as someone creating the world. For example, one cannot think of an eclipse without imagining that one has oneself put the sun and moon where they are.

When it comes to action, we have no real power at all, but that is what saves us morally. The application of reasoning to nature, even if it cannot ever be rigorous, is of moral importance and value: through it a man gets the idea of being a worker face to face with nature. Science gives us courage and makes men of us in so far it is real science.

2. In so far as reasoning does not apply to nature it allows us to invent series (a series of fluids more or less perfect, for example). In this sense, all deductions are hypothetical; they contain a perfection which is never found in the world. (One says: if the perfect fluid existed...)

This, on the other hand, has an obvious practical value.

As for its moral value, that is something very great: the world takes on an objective character, fixed, independent of us, of our passions. For example, the viscosity of a fluid can be something subjective, depending on the physical or moral state of the person who is deciding about it; once one has understood Archimedes' principle, this subjectivity no longer exists.

This is one of the two ways there are of delivering oneself from the passions: it comes about by means of the object, while the other way (mathematics) comes about through the subject. It is the way of the Stoics: any mind contemplating the world, succeeds in reaching the universal Mind.

This has its importance in the arts. (Examples: in music, the notes are determined in advance.)

So, scientific hypotheses give to the world the character of a work of art. The ancients had a very good understanding of this relationship that there is between science and aesthetics.

What is missing in deduction?

What is missing in it is always the world.

In no case can deduction take the place of verification. It is only what we start with. That is why people who only pay attention to mathematics end up by no longer seeing the value of mathematics.

Verification

Verification is not something which is straightforward. One might say that it is what is most difficult in science. It is what the Greeks failed at, and that for technical reasons, because apparatus has to be prepared in order to obtain data that can be measured. In order to arrive at a verification by means of an artificially set up experiment, one must start with hypotheses. The hypothesis is in the end confirmed by the verification.

What is of value in verification is that there is no thought in it; the power of thought is shown in the fact that it has to be voluntarily suspended once it recognises that what it lacks is the world.

Even if verification is something artificial, the experimenter draws aside as much as he can when he is face to face with the world, he is afraid of disturbing it. He has to have the kind of reserve towards it that the Stoics had.

The value of verification properly achieved is that the world is then seen as it is, without mind. For, what is of no use to men is an impure mixture of matter and mind (imagination).

In verification, one is able to set aside the divinity of the world and assign everything to mind.

Induction

It depends on two things:

1. The tendency which there is always in physics to generalise: one says: 'Water boils at 100 °C' as a sheep would say: 'Grass is good to eat.'

2. When induction gives rise to thought (one wants to find a relationship of cause to effect), it destroys itself, because the tendency then is to appeal to deduction. I try, for example, to find a deduction which would enable me to arrive at a boiling point of 100 °C. It is then that reasoning by analogy makes it appearance.

Reasoning by analogy

One cannot proceed from what is concrete to what is abstract.

As a result, one looks to see if it isn't possible, through analogy, to find another effect which has another cause, but which is of such a kind that the relationship of cause to effect is identical.

This is exactly the same thing as we have in Diophantus's rule of finding out whether something fits or not: we lay down something simple, and deduce from it something complex and, if we succeed in finding the relationship between this complex thing and what nature presents us with, then we have found an explanation of the phenomenon.

Examples: in the study of sound, one assumes an analogy between the waves which are made by a stone in water, and the 'crests' (nodes) and 'troughs' (anti-nodes): if I know the cause of the first phenomenon, then perhaps I shall be able to find out the cause of the second. We have the same thing in the study of light: just as motion+motion can produce rest, so light+light can produce darkness.

The real way of gaining knowledge about nature is to try to find analogies, so that the things which we do not bring about will appear as simple as those which we do (see Descartes).

Is there a method for finding analogies?

This is a difficult question: it looks as if it is a matter of intuition, of chance.

Let us look for examples in the history of sciences. One can say at once that analogies are assumed to exist between phenomena which resemble each other only in the way we understand them. That is obvious, for example, in the following cases:

reflection of light;
reflection of sound;
a ball rebounding from a wall.
(There is no resemblance in these cases: an echo is not at all like a mirror.)

an apple which falls;
the movement of the moon around the earth.
(One thinks that the moon falls on the earth, because it stays still, since it is assumed that it should move away from it.)

The whole of mechanics is based on the analogy between movements which do take place and ones that do not.

So, in order to find analogies, one has to do away with imagination, and only have recourse to the understanding.

Other examples: the pulley and the balance, the strap of a suitcase and the lever.

One has to isolate the essential relationships and get rid of everything accidental in order to see that these things are identical. Then the analogy is apparent, but the imagination has nothing to do with it. So, there must be an exercise of the understanding to get at the essential relationship as far as that as is possible. This is Descartes' rule II again: analyse the problem.

To sum up, the understanding can play a part in our knowledge of nature only through analogy, or rather the finding of analogies is the most important part the understanding plays in gaining knowledge of nature.

Nature provides us with data that are of a complicated kind; we have to assume analogies between these phenomena and in doing this we move from what is simple to what is complex.

What we obtain by analogy is essentially hypotheses; they are not true, but they are necessary if we are to have any knowledge of nature.

An hypothesis is a good one if it enables us to think clearly and to measure things. (For example, without Archimedes' principle, we have only confused thoughts of the phenomenon of bodies floating in water.)

Two conceptions of the experimental sciences

There is another conception of the experimental sciences in which analogy is absent. (Auguste Comte pointed out the opposition there is between these two methods.) This second method is applied when one makes separate measurements of data without knowing how they are related one to the other. In that case one ends up with 'functions', with algebra. One can, through algebra, establish analogies (electricity).

So we see that there are two ways of thinking of science: the first looks for simplicity, the second for unity.

These two ways may be opposed one to the other. At the present time, people look for unity above all else. Now, unity which does not give us any clear understanding is like an 'Open Sesame', it gives men power. And one has to choose between the Spirit and power, between God and Mammon. Men have chosen Mammon without any hesitation.

All the same, let us notice that, at all times, laws have been accepted without being understood and that, in our day, there have been attempts to explain them too. So it is a question of finding out which of these two methods will be the dominant one, rather than making a definite choice between the two of them.

Nevertheless there are other possibilities intermediate between these two; cases in which one can dispense with knowing what is happening. For example, one need not try to find out the mechanism by which heat is propagated (Fourier).[1] Archimedes, in studying the lever, did not ask himself why the whole lever moved at the same time, and not just the part on which the weight rested; he would have had to explain how the internal particles

[1] Joseph Fourier (1768–1830), French mathematician. His theorem states that any periodic oscillation (e.g. of light or sound) can be expressed as a mathematical series in which the terms are made up of trigonometric functions. See his *Analytical Theory of Heat*, trans. with notes A. Freeman (Cambridge University Press, 1878).

of a solid were arranged. In the same way, Descartes, when he studied reflexion, began by examining the movement of a ball against a wall; in this case too, he did now know why the ball did not embed itself in the wall.

We have the same thing in geometry; if one rotates a straight line one assumes that the straight line is a unity, one does not consider the intermediate points. Method is a matter of paying no attention to intermediate states. One is able to dispense with making hypotheses by doing this.

There are cases in which, by paying no attention to intermediate states, without appealing to any hypotheses, one can find clear and intelligible laws; there are other cases where this is quite impossible.

It is impossible, then, to talk of one method in experimental science; there are two which are interrelated.

Nevertheless, one can say that at Descartes' time science was rational and that today it is empirical. When one talks of the relationships between morality and science, one has to distinguish clearly between these two kinds of science. As is well understood, rational science also ends up with power. One doesn't have to oppose 'self-mastery' to 'mastery of the world'; what one has to do is to oppose 'the attempt to master oneself' to 'the attempt to gain mastery of the world'.

That is the meaning of what is said in the Gospel: 'Seek ye first the kingdom of God and his righteousness and all these things will be added unto you.'[1]

An examination of different theories and ways of considering the different experimental sciences

The quantum theory

It has brought a complete change in the ways mathematics and physics are related to each other.

---

[1] St Matthew's Gospel, 6.33. The Greek word translated 'righteousness' is *dikaiosune* and is translated into French as *justice*. In her essay 'Forms of the implicit love of God' (in *Waiting on God*, Fontana Books, London 1959) Simone Weil says that Christ taught that love of one's neighbour is justice.

The calculus of probabilities.

The discontinuous came into physics as a result of the discontinuous in chemistry. Chemistry is something discontinuous; it depends on classification. Chemistry – and so life – would be impossible without discontinuity.

Energy: this is at the centre of all physics. There are two laws which are more important than any others: 'conservation', 'entropy'.

A. An essential fact is: it is impossible to economise on the work done in simple machines. Throughout the centuries, people have sought for perpetual motion, that is to say, in fact, perpetual work. But the world would become something which one would no longer have to conquer once one discovered perpetual motion; it would then cease to be something real. The expressions 'kinetic energy' and 'potential energy' are different expressions for the same principle.

B. Further, it has been discovered that the work which is done is always less than that which should have been done. Research has been done on friction with the discovery that friction produces heat.

The second law ('entropy') is another way of saying that perpetual motion is impossible.

All these researches into energy are ruled by the saying: 'Man must work'. It is the saying: 'You will win your bread by the sweat of your brow'[1] stated in scientific terms.

Biology

It has two parts:

A. The study of living species and their relationships.

B. The study of organic functions.

Of course, these two studies are related to each other.

1. The theory of evolution (Lamarck) tells us: a living being tends to adapt itself, that is to say, to live. There is something like an 'occult quality' at work which hardly satisfies the mind.

2. Darwin's view is one we more easily accept. His system is a

[1] Genesis, 3.19.

rational reconstruction of the harmony we observe to exist between living beings and nature. The difficulty in his system has to do with continuity. In a word, a wing that is only just a little too weak for flight is of no use at all.

3. The theory of mutations was put forward to deal with this difficulty. The mutationists differed from Darwin in that they admitted abrupt changes (see Jean Rostand[1]).

The experimental means which have made the study of mutations possible are: (a) the study of hybrids; (b) the achievement of controlled environments in biology.

(a) The first mutationist was a Czech monk: Mendel.[2] What he discovered was: one brings about new varieties by bringing together varieties that already exist. Hybrids are always varieties of a quite definite kind: there are no small variations as Darwin thought.

(b) As for the controlled environment in biology, people who wished to show that Darwin was wrong discovered it. What they found out was that if one grows a plant in the ground and isolates it from what is outside it (for example from the insects which might have pollinated it) it spontaneously forms new varieties. All of a sudden, one doesn't know why, a plant of one variety gives a plant of another quite different variety. Now the plant cannot be called a 'hybrid' because one has isolated it. From this one comes to the conclusion that the changes come about by jumps.

Later a scientist[3] studied vinegar flies and discovered that the variations seemed to depend on certain yellow spots found in the primitive cell: the 'chromosomes'. So the idea arose that by altering the chromosomes one could make new species appear. But a technical means of altering chromosomes has not been found.

[1] Jean Rostand (b. 1894), French biologist, whose work was concerned with parthenogenesis. See his *L'evolution des espèces, histoires des idées transformistes* (Hachette, Paris 1932).

[2] Johann Mendel (1822–84), an Augustinian monk who spent most of his life teaching science, or as abbot, at Brnö, in what is now Czechoslovakia. C. D. Darlington says of him: 'His work, published in 1865, achieved as complete a public failure as it has been the lot of any discoverer to know.' See his *Genetics and Man* (G. Allen & Unwin, London 1964), pp. 88–101.

[3] Probably a reference to the work of Thomas H. Morgan (1866–1945), American biologist who was awarded the Nobel prize in 1933. See Darlington, *op. cit.*, pp. 108 ff.

Biology has become an experimental science only since the time of the mutationists.

An examination of what positive findings were made at each stage of advance in biology.

1. From Lamarck we keep the idea of evolution (species change).

2. From Cuvier: the idea of organic relationships. One sees the idea of relationship, in terms of harmony, applied to living beings. (Cuvier, for example, saw a jaw, and reconstructed a prehistoric animal.)

3. From Darwin, we keep the idea of conditions of existence. This most important idea of his has been forgotten; for people have seen in Darwin no more than the idea of evolution. It is that which has caught the imagination and excited people's passions.

Once the question of the mechanisms which governs the transmission of life has been placed aside, understanding a living being will amount to understanding how each of its organs, and the grouping together of all its organs, are necessary for the living being in the conditions in which it lives.

One has to try to rediscover the influence of the environment. To think of a living being as the end product of a process of evolution, is to move from what is simple to what is complex; for the understanding this must be thought of as a hypothesis. Once one has understood, for example, why the swallow has a slender beak, it is not any longer interesting to find out whether, as a matter of fact, the swallow twenty thousand years ago had a beak which was not as slender as it is now.

What this view of Darwin's leaves out is the idea of a state of equilibrium which leads to a discontinuity.

4. The school of mutationists has contributed the idea of living structures and that of an equilibrium based upon discontinuity. (To take an example: if we think of a dice, we see that there are six possible positions it can have, if thrown; the intermediate states do not exist because they are not states of equilibrium.) It is impossible that one organ alone should change because, if it does, the rest must change, and further, as we have seen, a wing either makes flight possible or it does not. That's quite definite. There aren't any transitions.

After this very quick examination, we can put forward the following definition: life is a certain combination, which, in the conditions determined by a given environment, brings about equilibrium.

Once one understands the organs are related one to the other, that there is an equilibrium, etc., one's thought is the same from a scientific point of view, whether one is a 'fixist' or 'evolutionist'.

The question of evolution is, on the whole, a matter of the imagination and the passions.

In the theories which are so violently opposed to one another, it is only the images that are different. As far as the understanding is concerned, the relationships are identical.

So one has to point out quite clearly that the question of evolution is not a real problem. One has only to pay attention and discover in each account relationships which are hidden by images.

We shall see that this is what needs to be done above all in sociology.

3

Politics and social theory

'Not to laugh at what human beings do,
nor to be disgusted by it, but to
understand it.' (Spinoza)

Sociology: how one is to think of it

Sociology is the last of the sciences in point of time. One might
say that it doesn't yet exist. Generally, people always deal with
social questions in such a way as to arouse passions. A scientific
study of society should enable us to see what kind of society it
is that would be the least oppressive in the given conditions. If
one could understand on what oppression depends, one would
no longer be in that unbearable situation of having to submit
to it by being forced in to a state of complete disorder. The
idea of inequality between the oppressors and the oppressed
would disappear. The oppressors would no longer think of themselves as the instruments of God; they would think of themselves as the tools of necessity. The oppressed, for their
part, would no longer think of the oppressors as a race set
apart.

Society does not depend on reason and virtue for 'religion holds
sway when a man is at the point of death, when diseases have
overcome the passions, and man lies lifeless, or else in temples
where men have nothing to do with one another; but it has no
power in the market place or at court, where its power is needed
most of all'. All men accept the most rigorous morality when there
is no question of putting it into practice. The coming of
Christianity, which brought with it the most pure morality in the
world, has brought no change at all.

The whole problem of politics comes to this: to find, in conditions as they are, a form of society which would conform to the

demands of reason and which at the same time would take into account necessities of a less important kind.

One has to begin by understanding the part played by this last kind of necessities.

A method as materialist as this is absolutely necessary if good intentions are to be changed into actions. It is absurd to want to reform society by reforming individuals.

How many individuals who are just and scrupulous in their individual lives do not hesitate to lie when they are diplomats, to exploit their workers when they are employers, etc.

A judge is dishonest while he is a judge, a doctor must lie, in order to reassure and to play the quack (in giving remedies which his patient would not admit he had given him). The worker, if he were to put on one side all the pieces of work he had botched, would not get enough to eat; so he passes them on to the next shift; then, when it is found out that the piece of work is botched, one doesn't know which worker to blame, so one cannot make the pay any less. In country markets it is the understood thing that both sides should haggle over the price. In paying taxes: one pays for oppression, prisons, machine guns, the secret police, lies of the press, etc.

The fact that men can do their jobs and still be human beings in their private lives shows that the profession puts blinkers over their eyes, that it canalises individual virtues and that individual virtues do not elevate the profession.

For all that, there are things which happen in society which no one wants: crises, for example. The very way society functions prevents men from being virtuous; it is a machine for making slaves and tyrants. It is a vicious circle: those who want to reform things mechanically end up in the pitiable way they have done in Russia; those who want to reform society by reforming individuals, have ended up with some very fine individual lives, but with nothing as far as society is concerned.

So one has to study society as one does biology, by studying the conditions of equilibrium.

The great sociologists

Auguste Comte

Auguste Comte is the founder of sociology. He invented the word.

His book on 'positive politics' is divided into 'social statics' and 'social dynamics'.

1. Statics is a study of the conditions which are common to all society without which a society would fall apart. These are: religion, in a very broad sense; property (in a very broad sense, too), thought of as being defined by each man's individual responsibility for the economic life; the family; language; government; the separation of powers (not in the sense of Montesquieu, but in the sense of the separation of temporal power from spiritual power).

The central idea of statics is that society depends on the conditions of production.

2. Dynamics is the study of change in society. It is much less precise than statics. Here is the scheme he put forward of the evolution of societies:

first form: theocratic societies (governed by priests);

second form: military societies: (a) a system based on attack (Sparta, Rome); (b) a system based on defence (the Middle Ages);

third form: industrial societies.

He makes some very good points, and goes into a lot of detail, but this succession he proposes has something abstract about it; it does not amount to a system.

Parallel to this, one should notice another development which Comte put forward: the three stages: (a) the theological; (b) the metaphysical; (c) the positive.

In the first of these, thunder is explained by reference to Jupiter. In the second, the gods are replaced by abstract beings. Comte used the word 'metaphysics' in a bad sense. (Examples: 'liberty', 'equality', in social questions, 'nature' in physics). In the third stage, one looks for laws.

The idea is that at any one particular time the different branches of thought are at different stages. For example, in the seventeenth century, history was at the theological stage (Bossuet)[1], medicine was at the metaphysical stage (the dormitive power of opium, occult qualities), the sciences at the positive stage. The important idea is: each branch of thought has to pass through the three stages.

Karl Marx

He had very definite views about the science of society.

Under determined conditions, a society is organised in such a way that it can continue to exist. A society is not determined by principles, but by its material conditions:

(1) the material environment;

(2) equipment – e.g. plant, tools, etc;

(3) the societies which surround it.

Each society is in conflict with nature and other societies, and so unless it is organised to survive, it will perish. So, throughout history, society is determined by material conditions.

This is exactly Darwin's idea. (Moreover Marx wanted to dedicate his book to Darwin, but Darwin refused.)

Let us give some examples:

1. Material environment: a people made up of sailors are not compelled to organise themselves as a people of peasants.

2. Equipment: a company armed with cannons will not be organised in the same way as one armed with bows and arrows.

3. Surrounding societies: if the opposing army is well disciplined it will be necessary that one's own is too; otherwise one is beaten in advance. (There is an analogy between society and an army.)

One should be able to give a complete account, at any given moment of history and in any given place, of the form of social organisation, without any appeal to ideas of virtue, goodwill, etc.

[1] Jean-Benigne Bossuet (1627–1704), French Roman Catholic bishop who influenced official religious policy in France during the reign of Louis XIV. (He was influential in Turenne's (see p. 99, note 1) ceasing to be a Protestant and becoming a Roman Catholic.)

Social oppression in history

The most important question is that of finding out what are the causes of social oppression.

Primitive societies

One has to point out that there have been societies where oppression has been very much less, where there were neither oppressors not oppressed. that is to say, where there were no classes. These are the societies called 'primitive'. For a long time it used to be thought that there were very powerful chiefs in these societies, but modern historical science has shown that the chief did not have any real authority. There were assemblies (for example, assemblies of 'Elders'), councils which arrived at decisions unanimously, not by a majority decision. We might think this extraordinary, but, in fact, when one considers that these men, who had no division of labour, had the same desires, the same life, etc. unanimity is something quite natural.

If one thinks about this for the first time, it would seem that societies of this kind would be the ideal. But, if we consider the matter more carefully, we see that a strongly democratic regime of this kind is related to very primitive forms of production. It is the oppression of nature that takes the place there of social oppression.

The priests and sorcerers, the only oppressors in these societies, represent that magical power which nature was considered to be by these 'savages'; they were subject to nature materially and morally. And then they became enslaved by other societies, once there were societies differently organised. (Example of the Germans once they came into contact with the Romans.)

So we must pass on to look at societies where there is oppression. It is a fact that all societies which know how to produce something are organised in an oppressive way.

Serfdom in Egypt

The first form of known oppression is serfdom (Egypt, Persia).

In Egypt, the life of the country depended on a system of irrigation due to the Nile. Now there is a difference between a man who lives by hunting and one who lives by irrigating his land; the hunter can hunt alone, but a peasant who lives on the banks of a river cannot build an isolated dyke at the edge of his field. So, we should not be surprised to find in Ancient Egypt a perfect example of state domination. On the other hand, wars were necessary to defend one's territory against those who wanted to gain possession of it, and also to gain possession oneself of other territories; for it is, of course, impossible to distinguish between offensive and defensive wars. (In fact, the best method of defending oneself, is to expand.) So one sees a caste of warriors appearing. And that is why Egypt was a military and feudal state.

But what was it that brought about serfdom?

Well, there has to be force exerted to complete long and exacting pieces of work like dykes, for in this case there is immediate need as there is in the case of the hunger that moves the hunter.

There must be a stable production for the ruling castes to be powerful. So they undertook these works.

The pyramids are a result of this system; it is very obvious that they were made without love, that they are the result of work undertaken by society as a whole.

So, beginning with Egypt, with its river Nile and its wars, one can rediscover the Egyptian state, in the same way as, beginning from the sea, and some other actual condition, one can arrive at fish.

Slavery in Greece and Rome

Slavery made its appearance in Greece.

It did not appear in Egypt because Egypt was not a maritime civilisation. Now, slavery depends on the seizure of slaves. But once one cannot carry off slaves one's interest turns to serfs.

The Cretan and Greek civilisations were completely maritime.

Think of their geographical form (isolated countries). If one does not take slaves into account, one finds in Greece the most democratic form of regime there is. The life of sailors cannot rest on traditions, the fragmentation of their life prevented a state-power from coming into existence. The result of this was the dawn of human thought. Nevertheless, this society was subject to its own laws.

Athens itself very quickly became what we should call an imperialist country (which Socrates denounced), then Greece went through a series of internal conflicts; at last came Alexander and the end of Greek civilisation.

In Rome we find slavery on a greater scale, and, for other reasons, we find there was no free thought there: there was not a single mathematician or physicist. The Romans were a people of peasants, not of sailors like the Greeks.

The power of Rome depended on its army, which was almost always at war, and so there had to be slaves, in those times, to work the land.

Rome made roads, ways of communication, (and that is the only contribution the Romans made to material civilisation). The roads (like the dykes in Egypt) were not an answer to any immediate need; so it is just a matter of realising that those who could make them were the most powerful.

Feudalism

Brigandage made production impossible; there was a state of disorder. Then, order was established by the brigands; and that was the regime of feudalism.

There had to be enough security for life to continue. Towns sprang up, where industrial work could be carried on. On the other hand, natural selection (the struggle of the lords among themselves) ended in the establishment of a monarchy, and a king was only a more powerful lord than the others.

One can look at the feudal regime as follows:

1. In war: then, it depended on trust, on voluntary obedience.

2. In the working of the lands: here there was almost unlimited

oppression. The peasants (the *jacqueries*[1]) revolted because they were hardly allowed enough to live on.

3. Among the workers in the towns: one cannot find workers who were less exploited than those of the Middle Ages. Civic virtues flourished, because each man thought that the city belonged to him.

One sees in this case an example of pure patriotism; serving one's native land without harming anyone else.

Why were the workers in the town in this privileged position? They were organised into guilds: it was a very fine period in which the love of work was the motivating force of production. The guild consisted of comrades working together. Production was founded on quality, and not on quantity.

Why this love of work – an image of which is to be seen in the cathedrals? The reason is, to a very great extent, that the worker had a clear idea of what his work was: he did not need anyone else to do any work for him. The love of making things played the role then that is now played by coercion (motive for work).

The theoretical problem of oppression

After examining these actual examples, we go on to deal with the problem of oppression from a theoretical point of view.

Definition of oppression: it is the negation of Kant's principle. Man is treated as a means.

To find out how it is possible to try to get rid of oppression, or at least to make it less, one has first of all to put the following questions:

A. Its positive side.

What is there in oppression which makes it into a weapon of defence against nature and against men?

1. Unity of action.
Cf. Homer: 'The rule of the many is not good, one ruler let there be.'

Goethe: 'One mind is enough for a thousand hands.'

Any work, if it is to be effective, must be co-ordinated. Now, all

---

[1] *Jacqueries*: the French peasant revolts were given this name. The best known is the one that broke out in 1358 which was ruthlessly put down.

co-ordination is related to the intelligent activity of a mind. This is an undeniable law. It holds good in the struggle against nature, and in the struggle against men. Nature will not allow centralisation in action to increase indefinitely; the struggle against nature is limited, that against men has no limits.

2. Distinction between 'those who superintend action' and 'those who act'. Due to this human forces can reach extreme limits (war – mines – aviation: cf. *Night Flight* by Saint-Exupéry[1]).

Man, in fact, does not know the limits of his powers. To achieve some kind of limit there has to be constraint. This distinction then, succeeds in accomplishing impossible things, miracles.

3. Limitation of consumption.

The principle of material progress is to produce means of production and not of consumption (roads, bridges, machines).

Men, when no constraint is put on them, show no self-denial. (A simple example from fishing: if one did not limit fishing, there would soon be no more fish – so laws and police are necessary to protect the fishermen against themselves.)

The division between the exploiters and the exploited necessarily sets a limit to consumption, for if the exploited consume (illegally that is) they are put in prison.

(The example of the forests in the Middle Ages: there were dreadful punishments for those who stole wood.)

Today, what would happen, for example, if a war exhausted mineral resources?

The mining companies who, quite obviously, are companies of exploiters, set a high price on coal; that preserves the coal mines.

So, from this point of view, monopoly capitalism is the guardian of the wealth of society.

B. Its destructive side.

Now, is there something negative, destructive in oppression?

1. From a material point of view.

Competition among oppressors – military war or economic

---

[1] Antoine de Saint-Exupéry (1900–44), French aviator and writer, whose novel *Night Flight* is a story about a dangerous flying mission. (Trans. Stuart Gilbert, Desmond Harmsworth, London 1932.) Saint-Exupéry himself died during World War II on a flying mission.

competition – publicity: what efforts are wasted in advertising! It is the same kind of thing with armaments; one makes a little more because one's enemy has done so; there is no limit (and that is one of the causes of crises).

2. From an intellectual point of view.

(a) The separation there is between thought and the world: in fact, those who think, belong to a privileged class; the workers do not have the leisure time to think. All culture is, in this way, made into something false.

(b) Thought subject to authority: whenever the oppressors realise that thought is something they cannot control, they put it down, (by hemlock, by the cross.) There have been two periods which are exceptions to this law: the great period of Greek thought (which nevertheless did not possess a feeling for the world, the presence of nature) and the period of the Renaissance (Descartes).

3. From a moral point of view.

Oppression is an insult to the dignity of human nature.

C. In what direction is salvation to be sought?

Now that we have seen the destructive side of oppression, let us see if it is possible to restate in some other way its three positive advantages. First of all, one has to admit that one cannot deny their existence (we have seen this in studying the society of savages: otherwise one is delivered up to nature, to superstition.)

1. Unity of action: is there some way of achieving it other than that of oppression?

If we think in terms of a necessity that must govern us, we have to say that it does not bring about a stable unity. It is thought which creates unity. So, if, for example, all the sailors knew the purpose of the captain's orders, they would be in a good position to see whether they must be accepted. In any case they would not be slaves.

2. Pressure on human beings.

In this case, there must be before everything else a motive for work. Workers give themselves to some piece of work when they understand it. So, if the way the work is to be done and the principle which governs it are understood by each of the workers, they will be the real creators of the work.

3. Limitation of consumption.

It comes about quite naturally.

So, it is a matter of ensuring that the workers work knowing what they are doing; of giving to the workers controlling power over the whole of production. (N.B. not in the way this has been done sometimes in Germany.)

D. Our duties in relation to social phenomena.

Above all it is necessary not to ignore their existence. One can give money to the unemployed, but that doesn't stop them from being unemployed; one can do the same for miners, but that doesn't mean that they no longer have to face the threat of death due to fire-damp; one can give one's attention to the children of the workers, but that will not mean that they will find work when they leave school, etc.

It is quite impossible to avoid the social problem. The first duty that it places on one is not to tell lies.

The first form of lie is that of covering up oppression, of flattering the oppressors. This form of lie is very common among honest people, who in other ways are good and sincere, but who do not realise what they are doing. Human beings are so made that the ones who do the crushing feel nothing; it is the person crushed who feels what is happening. Unless one has placed oneself on the side of the oppressed, to feel with them, one cannot understand.

A second kind of lie is demagogy.

These two faults are serious ones.

They are faults committed by honest people, but it also happens that they take on a hideous character. For example, with regard to the first kind of lie, there are people who make it their job to flatter oppressors; those in power always find people who spend their lives in praising and flattering those who spill blood. Nine journalists out of ten, optimists that they are, have taken up this job of telling lies on behalf of the oppressors.

As for the second kind of lie, think of the bureaucrats in workers' organisations, whose job is to make the oppressed believe that their freedom will be achieved overnight. It matters not a jot to them to see the workers killed by the police, if that serves their propaganda purposes.

So, the first thing to be done is to rebut these two kinds of lie. One has to state the facts, and not to hide from anyone that millions of people are crushed by the social machine; one has to find out the causes, not only of oppression in general, but of such and such oppression in particular, then find ways of making it less if one can. One should only advise the oppressed to revolt if it can be successful. It doesn't often happen that one can find things to do the results of which are perfectly clear. So, when one is in the position of supposing that a number of different courses of action are equally likely to succeed, one has to depend on inspiration, like Descartes' traveller in the forest.

Economic life and the way it works

History and science

We shall first tackle the question of history.

Is history a science?

1. Generally speaking, history is scientific when it depends on documents whose accuracy is not questioned.

But, as things are, it is difficult to find out the truth. There are distortions due to corruptions in the text, to prejudice, etc. There are periods of which we can know next to nothing (Egypt), others about which there is no shortage of documents and information which contradict each other. One has to take into account falsifications, to study the life of the writer, his passions, his interests, etc.

2. But, once one has thoroughly examined that, once one has pieces of information of which one is certain, it is necessary to establish relationships between the facts, to establish laws. 'Laws are the necessary relationships established by the nature of things.'

One would have to establish this idea for history to be a science. History then becomes a part of sociology. ('Social dynamics' of Marx.)

The historical understanding of social evolution

Our aim is to find out whether one can conceive of a scientific explanation, that is to say, one that is necessary, of social changes.

Tacitus, Sallust, Livy,[1] are historians who all tell stories of their own. But, the greater historians are, the deeper is the grasp of the social reality of the times in which they lived that one finds in them. Tacitus, for example, shows very well the part played by the army as a collective whole. But, they did not consciously set out to do this kind of thing.

Bossuet was the first person to attempt to show that there is a continuity in human history. The principle of the continuity, for him, is God.

In the eighteenth and nineteenth centuries history is dominated by the idea of progress (exception: Rousseau). It was a universal world spirit that concerned Voltaire and the Encyclopaedists. What could be the driving force of progress? Good will on the part of human beings. They took it for granted that Frederick the Great or Catherine the Great (enlightened despotism) would bring progress about. It was a very naive idea.

In the nineteenth century progress appeared as a self-perpetuating force, a tendency within societies to adapt themselves to a form which suited them (cf. Lamarck). That came to an end in 1914.

The idea of progress took on new life from 1923 to 1929 during a time of prosperity. There was a general feeling that the social problem was going to solve itself (Ford).

The present century did not become aware of itself without a crisis. Historical questions were necessarily put in a new way; the aim was to get rid of this mythological idea of progress.

After this introduction to the question, let us take it up again in more detail, with reference to Auguste Comte and Karl Marx.

Auguste Comte's view

Humanity moves from what is lower to what is higher according to a law of its own. We have already seen his idea of three stages. That is just one example of his general view of things. His slogan was: 'order and progress'. Order is foundation of progress.

[1] Tacitus (*c*. A.D. 55–120), Sallust (86–35 B.C.), Livy (59 B.C.–A.D. 17), Roman historians.

Understanding him in this way, conservatives and even reactionaries have been influenced by him (Maurras[1]). But his idea of progress is different from that of the eighteenth century which Comte would have taken to be 'metaphysical'.

One does not completely leave the lower stage behind in passing to the higher one. (Example: one still uses the standards of military life at the industrial stage.)

Comte founded the religion of humanity. He called himself its high priest; he thought that after his time there would be an immediate change to the positive stage. Nevertheless Comte still had this mystical idea of inevitable progress. (Let us note that it is perhaps impossible to try to live in society without this idea. But this idea, which is a guide to action, must be distinguished from scientific thought.)

Karl Marx's view

With the materialist method, we come to something more definite. But Marx's teaching is a very strange mixture of scientific views and metaphysical beliefs.

Marx's view is that the structure of society depends on the conditions of production, that there are in each society class struggles which depend on the conditions of production, and that, depending on the changes of these conditions, such and such a class will dominate.

But how are these conditions of production to be changed?

There are, sometimes, changes due to natural disasters, but they happen less and less often. The change of the conditions of production has to be looked for in the changes of the relationships that exist between man and nature.

This becomes more complicated, because inversely, the relationships between man and nature depend on the forces at work in society itself. Marx resolved the problem by saying that the forces of production progress. So, after having tried to get rid of the mythological idea of human progress, he reintroduced it in the forces of production, and this is even less conceivable. Auguste

[1] Charles Maurras (1868–1952), French writer who was given a life sentence of solitary confinement for his collaboration with the Nazis.

Comte had already said: 'The silent influence of the dead more and more rules the lives of the living.'

Now each generation prepares the world for its children, but also uses up natural resources (land and sources of energy). So Marx's view does not hold. Marx was influenced by his belief in progress; his generous nature made him burn with the desire to set the oppressed free; so much so that his belief in progress went beyond the bounds of objective judgement, and what is more, he lived at a time of prosperity and he accepted the illusions of his age.

There is, in Marx, something else mythological: the confusion between the idea of economic progress and moral progress.

The mission or historical task of each regime is to prepare the way for the one that comes after it. So, capitalism prepared the way for socialism. (If equality is to have sense it has to be equality in welfare.) Capitalism increased the forces of production. Marx believed that the old age of capitalism had already come in his time. 'The bourgeoisie brings into being the diggers of its own grave' (the proleteriate). After that, will come the higher stage of communism. Men would no longer wear themselves out, but work at their pleasure and consume as much as they please. 'From each according to his ability, to each according to his needs', that is the formula of the kind of society of the higher stage of communism. Men would be completely free: of law, of the state, of any kind of constraint.

What we have here is a messianic attitude of mind which generally never goes with science, and which is quite mythological. It is this which forces the communists to put off forever the time when their state will be achieved, since, in any case, they will eventually win (just like God when he is thought of as some external power).

Property

We agree that societies change with the run down of their means of production.

In the Middle Ages, the most important thing that happened was probably the exhaustion of the land – the result of this was

an excess population of agricultural workers, since a balanced state
of affairs had not yet been achieved. Then, this gave rise to a
movement towards to the towns, and a new phenomenon is seen:
trade guilds come to an end. Among the rich merchants there were
those whose only aim was to employ men for the smallest possible
sum. And that was the end of organised guilds.

So one has the beginning of the exploitation of work. It is from
this time that money began to bear interest in economic life itself.
Let us imagine what could happen to a master-tradesman, together with his partners in business, who became rich and opened
a somewhat bigger workshop. This would result in even more
division of labour, more rationalisation. The difference between
the production of a group of eight workers and a group of four
will go to the employer.

But if the 'partners in the business' possess the whole business,
then the workers would go on possessing less and less.

The money gained by the worker in the workshop would be less
than the difference in value between the manufactured article and
the raw material. The worker himself would end up as a
commodity for sale.

How is the price of this new merchandise decided? By the
worker? Well! The law of supply and demand will play its part
here as elsewhere, and the profit of the employer is the difference
between the price of the manufactured goods and the amount paid
to the worker. So the nature of property has completely changed.
Earning wages is nothing but another form of slavery, but with
this difference: slaves were obtained by pillage, and the wage
earners by commercial agreement.

But capitalist property finds itself in a state of contradiction as
a result. At the present time, real property no longer exists. The
bankers do what they want with the money. No one can work
enough to possess capital in the form of money. Those who do
not have enough money to take over someone else's property, can
no longer have control of their own. Today it is the banks that
control industry. (Ford is an exception.) Citroen belongs to the
banks, who put them back into business. The banks force industrialists into bankruptcy; they then lay down their own conditions:

they control the industrialists. If an industry has its back against the wall, that is to say has no credit, any bank which takes it over will be able to lay down its own conditions. Bourgeois property is something that no longer exists.

Those who have control of ten thousand francs in a bank are the owners of ten thousand francs which belong in name only to someone else.

As a result of this self-aggrandisement real property has ceased to exist. At the moment property is based on usurpation.

How can money yield interest?

In the Middle Ages, the main source of profit was war (pillage). Then later it was work: at first a worker possessed what he produced. Nowadays it is quite the opposite; a worker in a shoe factory can go around in bare feet. Last of all, there was usury, which is an act of violence. The church in the first centuries of our era recognised it as such, and condemned it outright.

Nowadays, money gains interest all by itself in banks without one's needing to work. That is something quite strange. How can that happen? The first economists believed that profit was the result of trade: one makes money, without stealing or working, by selling things for more than they are worth. But this explanation becomes absurd once one extends it to the whole world of industry and trade. If one increases prices by a fifth all round, nothing is changed.

So, the problem arises afresh. The increase in money has got to come from somewhere.

Well, there is a misunderstanding about the work-market. The worker is selling himself: the employer buys the worker as a producer. The worker can always produce more than the equivalent of what he consumes. If the worker possessed what he produced and sold it for what it was worth, it would be quite different. The worker works only partly to support himself; he also works gratis to support his employer.

Economic power

But what forces the workers to sell themselves? We have to examine more closely what makes the employer rich.

Economic power is something comparatively new. Previously, power was above all something military (serfs, slaves). Military power became economic power once there was big industry. This change can be seen quite clearly in the literature of the seventeenth century (Saint Simon[1]: 'Visit of the Banker to Louis XIV'); there is a change from individual to collective production.

Let us note that this is a matter of degrees; transport has always been something collective (roads); the unity of the state depends on that.

All the same, for the most part, work had been something individual up to the time of the coming of capitalism. The peasants were tenants of the land which they could cultivate, the craftsman owned his own tools and materials.

Collective work and method

There is a state of enslavement to tradition: secrets that belong to the job, the routine of peasant life. As long as one trusts to instinct one cannot do any collective work, because different people's instincts are not the same: work became collective once it became systematic.

There has been more and more a division of labour.

In the end, we have 'specialised' workers. This is an application of Descartes' rule to divide up the difficulties.

But, if method makes its appearance in the work, it no longer exists in the worker.

One plus one cannot make two except in the mind of one man by himself. Action that is unified in a systematic way cannot exist in the case of a single worker, but only for the person who directs the whole body of workers.

At the same time the sciences and the mining industries deve-

[1] Saint-Simon (Louis de Rouvroy) (1675–1755), French writer whose famous *Memoirs* cover a part of the reign of Louis XIV. Trans. Bayle St John (Samuel Bagster & Son, London 1902).

loped. In the first instance scientists had invented machines as playthings.

The causes of big industry are:

1. an abundant supply of iron at a reasonable price (the use of coal for the mining of iron ore; blast furnaces);

2. the development of ideas in mechanics;

3. the division of labour to its furthest limits.

In big industry, the opposition between a systematic and a blind way of working becomes quite clear: even the co-ordination is entrusted to a computer (machines). Method is taken away from men and transferred to matter.

Once that has happened, men become cogs in a machine. The workers have in actual fact become things in their own work.

Big industry and the firm

Marx's[1] formulae: 'Among craftsmen who work by hand, the worker uses his tools; in the factory he is at the service of the machine. In the former case it is the worker himself who has control of the instruments used in work, whereas in the latter he has to follow the movements of the machines. In craftsmanship the worker's limbs formed a living machine; in the factory, there is dead machinery which is independent of the workers, of which they are part like living cogs in a machine.'

'What belongs to the individual destiny of the unskilled factory worker is of no account in the face of science, powerful natural forces and collective work. For all these become crystallised in the system of the machine and are part and parcel of the owner's power.'

'Capitalism is the subordination of living work to dead work... It is a reversal of the ordinary relationship between subject and object.'

What relation does the owner have to these machines? He is as much their slave as the worker is.

[1] Karl Marx (1818–83). See, for example, his *Grundrisse* (The Pelican Marx Library, Harmondsworth 1973), pp. 767–78, and Simone Weil's late essay, 'Is there a Marxist doctrine?' in *Oppression and Liberty*, (Routledge & Kegan Paul, London 1958).

What is essential about the domination which crystallises itself in big business is the way in which the individual becomes subordinated to the collectivity. The power of the capitalist is the power of machines over the workers, while, in the manufacturing process the owners do nothing but co-ordinate the work.

The laws which govern big business: quite generally, the law which governs all power is competition. Here it is economic competition. (We refer to production, not to the power of exchange.) Power which is based on collective organisation cannot be maintained except by extending the collective organisation. The big firm will always oust the smaller one. One has to take on more workers and introduce a greater division of labour.

So the free work of the workers goes in fact to the firm, not to the owner. It is the firm which extorts work gratis from the workers. The firm buys dead tools and living ones. Thanks to the fact that it is in the nature of the living tools to produce more than they consume the firm expands.

Nowadays, the employer must, if he is to gain credit, appear rich; luxury is, for the employers, a way of showing their power and making it greater. In Russia the employer is gone, but the factory is still there. It makes no difference. The law which governs economic life as it is, is accumulation of wealth. The employer has the power to think only of himself, but no power to be good.

So, what is central in this problem is big industry and not the institution of property. The interests of those who represent the power of the firm and of those who work are absolutely opposed to one another.

It is not a question of what form of government there is, but what form of productive system exists. The state is for all practical purposes in the hands of the capitalists.

In Russia, it is at bottom exactly the same.

Social life itself changes at the same time as economic life. The way in which work is co-ordinated has got the better of methods of production. The same is true of the state as a whole.

Bureaucracy

The present form of the state with its bureaucracy reflects the primary role played by co-ordination. Bureaucrats do nothing except co-ordinate what other people do. They tend to become parasites, to increase beyond what is necessary. That happens because it is impossible to control them and because bureaucracy is something that works like a machine (limited companies).

Whether it be a dictator or a king, he will depend on the bureaucracy (Stalin).

This apparatus has instruments of its own which are themselves collective in character: the army, the police become bureaucracies.

The helplessness of the individual

So, the individual counts for almost nothing at all. It is difficult to explain how this has come about because of the way people have had the wool pulled over their eyes in the last sixty years. The individual has no recourse against anyone. If the police molest him, he has no protection. The press is in the hands of the police. The police if they want to can make an innocent man guilty.

The magistrates, the civil service, these are meant to serve the citizens, but when the citizens have some complaint to make they have no effective way of making it.

The present state of affairs

Workers are nothing but 'things' on the labour market

Wage earners are treated like things on the labour market because they are bought and sold there and also because of the rate at which they are bought.

In order to be in the favoured position of being able to sell themselves for that price they have even to buy over the foreman.

We have only to think of the docks at Marseilles, of the women who are forced to sell themselves so that their rickety children can live – miserable beings who before long will undergo the very same slavery.

Unemployment benefit only comes with a slump. Apart from

that nothing is done for the unemployed. The workers are treated much worse than Cato's slaves; even able-bodied young men are thrown to the rubbish heap.

Workers as 'things' in big business

Workers are again treated as things when they are no longer out of work, and have entered a firm.

There with 'rationalisation', assembly line work, their lives are forever sacrificed (conveyor belts, buildings, mines). What is more, especially in America, the workers are often watched in their private lives. (Ford: they employ informers.)

Why all this? Because the machines need men less than men need machines. Men are now the slaves of machines. That is something Descartes never foresaw in his *Discourse on Method*. Nature dominates man now through the machine. Those who are masters of the machines are masters of men and of nature. They have even chosen to be the perpetrators of this oppression.

Palliatives?

Palliatives have been tried often enough.

1. Capitalists like Ford: the workers have a share in benefits handed out; this is nothing but a way of corrupting them. It is a bonus for producing more, a cause of the workers demeaning themselves even more.

2. Socialist parties: works councils; so-called participation of workers in the way the firm is run. It has changed nothing at all.

3. Russia: the capitalists have been driven out. That only goes to prove that it is no use doing that as long as big industry survives. The capitalists are replaced by bureaucrats.

4. Workers' syndicates (Germany – Italy – Austria): one can scarcely speak of them yet.

Their plans worked out on paper are not very precise. A situation like this cannot be changed by some palliative, but only by a transformation of the means of production.

Coercion: the 'rights of men' are trampled under foot

The political consequences of such a state of affairs: our social system depends on coercion. The workers submit to it but they cannot accept it. Coercion does not go with democracy. It is obviously quite impossible for men to be treated like things in the labour market and in production and to be treated as citizens in public life.

In effect, freedom of expressing one's views is subordinated to the capital of machines; there are things which cannot be said in bourgeois newspapers, nor any longer in the newspapers which appeal to workers, because one is not orthodox.

There is no real freedom of speech (it is difficult to hire a room, to stick up notices, etc.).

There is no personal freedom: one faces prison, an unjust sentence.

As for the magistrates, the rich can buy them; they threaten them with a campaign in the press, or promise them political support. Just to get the services of an advocate, one has to have money.

Besides, everything has to be bought at a price. One cannot go to war without money; the mines at Briey[1] were not bombed although they provided the Germans with mineral resources throughout the war. All the laws guaranteeing freedom and equality in the Republic are illusions because the state is not controlled nor can it be.

It is impossible to bring about a reform of the state unless one first of all changes the system of production.

It is very easy to see that the more the mass of workers are oppressed by the economic regime, the more oppressive the state becomes. And if one thinks of a totalitarian state, one form of oppression only brings another with it. When it is the same power which dominates big business and everything else, one is completely helpless: that is what it's like in Russia.

'Fascist' states are on the way to the same thing.

In France there is still some freedom left.

[1] Briey – industrial town in North-West France near the border with Germany.

Duties towards the state

1. Towards the state as it is.

It is a brute force; obedience is a necessity not a duty. Or rather, one has a duty towards oneself not to knock one's head up against the brick wall of the state when it can serve no purpose. On the other hand, one has a duty, and not a right, never to let one atom of the liberty which the state allows to disappear; never to accept official ideology, but to create centres of independent thought. One has a duty to fight against the oppression of the state in so far as doing this does not result in suicide.

2. Duties to change the state.

We are going to look at a number of different views of this.

Different views of the state

Machiavelli [1] (in *The Prince*)

A ruler has to promise less than he can fulfil, do what is evil all at once, but distribute any benefits in small doses. A ruler has to make his subjects feel that they depend upon him all the time. He should think of nothing else except war and military exercises. A ruler must know no fear, and show his liberality not secretly, but for everyone to see. He is more certain to be feared than loved; for love is a good which men destroy if they will it; while they are held in terror by fear.

By making war abroad, revolution at home is avoided.

The ruler must, at definite times of the year, keep the people occupied with feasts and entertainments.

Machiavelli made force and law completely separate from one another. Tyrants defend themselves for the most part by quite deliberately confusing force and law. We have to be grateful to Machiavelli for making this analysis. His cynicism shows force pure and simple; that the essence of authority is fear on the part of the subjects, and cruelty on the part of the rulers.

---

[1] Nicolo Machiavelli (1469–1527). See *The Prince*, trans. W. K. Marriott (Everyman's Library).

Rousseau[1]

His view is quite different. He gives us a picture of what a perfect society based on the free consent of each person would be. Of course it cannot be realised because men are not good.

The origin of the social contract: natural necessity.

But one has to find a form of association which injures no one; that means 'finding a form of association through which each person, uniting together with everyone, nevertheless is subject to no one except himself'. (This defines the whole social problem.) Each accepts the will of all in advance. This acceptance marks the change from the state of nature to a state or civilised society. The existence of society is the condition of exercising reason, according to Rousseau's view.

Rousseau's view in brief:

Once laws are seen to be obligations which the citizens contract with one another, there must be a state of perfect mutual agreement between the society and the citizens; all the citizens must be related to the society in exactly the same way.

It is impossible to entrust the direction of the people to anyone else except the people themselves.

There must be no deliberation except on matters about which the people are unanimous.

If the whole people are going to be unanimous in dealing with things, all the subjects must join in action together; they must not just be part of affairs as inert objects.

All the citizens have to play an equally active part in collective action, that is in production.

Decisions about the public good must not be made by private individuals. It is a sad thing to have to say: the 'social contract' exists at the level of an ideal. There is nothing real about it.

Marx and Lenin

The state machine is made up of civil servants (the bureaucracy), the army, the police. It is a machine for oppression. The army,

[1] Rousseau, *The Social Contract*, trans. G. D. H. Cole (Everyman's Library).

the police and the bureaucracy are always there. As long as three institutions of this kind exist, there will be oppression. What the Russians have experienced shows this only too well. Marx wanted a militia to take the place of a standing army. (There should be no professional soldiers.) The militia would be made up of citizens who, together with the person who is their chief, do military service occasionally. He wanted a police force controlled by the people. Lenin wanted responsible people, answerable for what they do, who receive the same payment as skilled workers, to take the place of the bureaucracy. In that case, people would all have to take their turn at it.

These measures are in complete agreement with the 'social contract', for all these people would consider things as citizens and not as members of the government. They would know that two years later they would be subject as citizens to the measures they had taken. All the illusions of power would be reduced to a minimum, and the maximum amount of objectivity of judgement would be realised. No amount of good will can be a substitute for this. The more permanent some power is, the more oppressive it is.

Nowadays, for all practical purposes, the powers that be are permanent. It is a matter of doing away with this kind of oligarchy. Can such an institution be destroyed and what conditions are necessary to achieve this?

The delegates of the people (and delegates are necessary, since the people do not have the time to govern themselves) must be from the people, and not stop belonging to it in exercising their public powers.

So one has to find out: 1. whether this view has justice on its side; 2. whether it can be practised.

There are two views about this: (a) government for the people, but not by the people; (b) government for the people and by the people.

The first of these is 'enlightened despotism'.

Enlightened despotism

The despot's interests lies in allowing his subjects only a limited form of freedom and happiness. Can a despot be so just that he only considers the interests of his subjects? The more a man trusts in his own ability, the stronger and more powerful he will become. Now, to do good for one's subjects, is to increase their power to act. So one cannot increase it if one starts off by taking it away. Political power alienates human beings, whom we assume to have a body and imagination, from a common life. And last, but not least, all people have feelings and like to give orders for the sake of giving orders; this delight in having the upper hand is very likely to destroy all decent thoughts and intentions.

Whenever there is a monopoly of power those who are in power are our enemies. One doesn't have to overthrow by violence and with no hope for the future; one has to try to limit their power just as one tries to stop invaders in time of war.

So it makes little difference what kind of power it is, as long as it is a monopoly. The monopoly of power is something which has been firmly established ever since there have been nation states.

'All political revolutions have had the same effect; they have done nothing except bolster up the state machine instead of destroying it' (Russia); what Marx expected has been confirmed only too well.

The second view (government by the people and for the people) is that of a republic.

A republic

A republic only destroys this monopoly on paper, but not in reality; the reason for this is that public offices are treated as careers; and there is a permanent body of people who have them in their grasp. The 'servants of the state' are its masters.
How to do away with this monopoly?

One has to do away with those features of public offices which people find attractive by making the salaries they get smaller. It is also necessary to ensure that there are different people filling them continually (Lenin). There must be a system of rotation in these jobs.

But the monopoly that exists in offices depends on a monopoly of abilities. That is why 'every cook should learn how to govern'.

Co-operatives, worker syndicates must be founded and bureaucracy avoided. But that is difficult to achieve. A man stays secretary if he is the only one with sufficient intellectual ability and so there is a vicious circle. He doesn't try to instruct his comrades; and there we have in miniature what goes on in the state at large.

This idea has further ramifications: no offices which serve society as a whole should be a monopoly (as economic life is). An artificial separation is thus made between economic and political life. Nowadays it is office, and not property, which creates economic power. Economic power is defined by the administration. The monopoly of economic and political functions are related. Economic and political democracy should go hand in hand, or there is no democracy at all. For example, if a worker were director of a factory for one year, and the jobs changed hands regularly, there would be direction not oppression.

Theoretically that is fine; but can it be put into practice? The workers would have to have a sound theoretical education.

In the meantime, the state is an evil oppressor and one has to do one's best to make the evil as little as possible.

There are four ideas to be looked at:

1. a democratic state
2. a completely co-operative state
3. a monarchy
4. a fascist state.

A democratic state

There are still some unknown liberties in Germany or in Russia. What there is is very precious indeed. These liberties are connected with economic life. A crisis necessarily brings with it reinforcement of authority.

A completely co-operative state

The main idea is that one has to prevent the state bringing about a totalitarian state of affairs.

But is that possible?

The workers' representatives are forced to obey the state. If the state, in fact, succeeds in extending its economic power through trade unions, that will inevitably mean that its political powers will be increased. But there are degrees here: the less control the state has over trade unions, the less evil is the organisation of the system.

Monarchy

Decentralisation – but, at the present time, there is an overriding necessity about it, one must not have any illusions about it (the Bolsheviks, the Jacobins). All the same, one has to try the lesser evil.

Separate Councils; these depend on the king. (In this they are opposed to trade unions.)

An improvement in the conditions of agricultural workers in order to stop the exodus for the towns.

Right to strike for economic reasons, not for political ones.

No limitation in number of working hours.

In fact the state is all-powerful through the monarch.

This is rule through powers that are legally established; that is what is fundamental to it, as well as its view of responsibility as something individual, not collective. The monopoly of public offices is made into a principle (and this is the very opposite of Marx's view).

Comment: at the present time there is too much for one man to deal with, in particular if we take into account the whole of industry and finance. If the aim is to bring about unity, no one man could do it all. Individual powers and responsibilities are impossible, just as much as individual control is. So what will have to be done is to find a way of decentralising economic life. There are things which favour this: electricity.

Capitalist enterprises, once the power of controlling them is no longer possible for one man, become swamped by bureaucracy.

A fascist state

Mussolini.

Complete centralisation.

The driving force of the system, from a moral point of view, is devotion, sacrifice, the complete denial of oneself. Life is thought of as a struggle. One must despise life's conveniences. Apart from the march of history, man is nothing. 'For fascism, everything belongs to the state, and nothing human or spiritual is of any importance and *a fortiori* there is nothing which has value apart from the state. Fascism raises itself above the antithesis: "monarchy/republic". What is cultivated is the myth of the general interest. The end is society, the species, the collectivity. "The state is the absolute in which the individuals and groups are only relative." The state is the will to power and domination.'

Comment: that is the secret intention of every state. All power tends in the direction of making itself greater. The state has natural tendency to be totalitarian. That is seen everywhere.

Russia

The same idea is central there: 'the individual counts for nothing'. Complete sacrifice, even of one's moral conscience. Cf. Victor Serge's book: *La Ville conquise.*[1] The conclusion is: 'We are nothing, the masses are everything, we have to sacrifice everything to the mass, even our scruples.'

But who profits from this sacrifice? At first, one might say: 'the working class'. Now it is the state. The state has become more and more the expression of the working class. The individual is denied everything for the profit of the state. Internationalism turns into nationalism.

Features that are common to Germany, Italy, Russia: a morality of devotion, denial, not only in connection with pleasures, but also with regard to peace of mind. Even the person who is at the head

[1] Victor Serge (1890–1947), *Ville Conquise* (Reider, Paris 1932). See his *Memoirs of a Revolutionary* (1901–41) trans. P. Sedgwick (Oxford University Press, London 1963), and *Birth of our Power* trans. Richard Greeman (Victor Gollancz, London 1968).

does not pursue comfort, but power. These features are much more obvious in Russia than in any other state.

This morality of devotion is put at the service of the police. In point of fact, everyone is part of the police. The main way of going about things is to capture the youth. The state controls them from the age of seven; they have to wear uniform. There is no homework, no lessons at home. The school is given over to the 'pioneers', who in the last resort have the say over the school teachers. The young are told to denounce members of the teaching staff and their parents. Competitions are organised; the winner is the one who converts his parents most quickly. This attempt to capture the young is completely anti-marxist.

There is one party; one party in power and all the rest are in prison. When there is a majority in this party the minority are thought to be a break-away party (Trotsky[1]). There is only one press, one literature. Marx and Lenin are subversive in Russia. Education belongs exclusively to the state, even in matters that would seem to be independent of it (biology[2]). In Russia, in addition to all the propaganda and fanaticism there is industrialisation.

Conclusion: the state is the worst of all evils.

The right practical attitude towards the state

After this examination let us try to give a better definition of duties towards the state.

It is assumed that some functions of the state are in the interest of everyone; one has the duty in respect of these functions to accept what the state imposes with good grace. (Example: regulation of traffic.)

---

[1] Simone Weil once met Trotsky during the year she was teaching at Roanne and she arranged for her parents to allow him to hold a meeting at their home. (Trotsky had been allowed into France on condition that he held no meetings.) She is said to have disagreed violently with his views, so much so that Trotsky said to her: 'If that's how you think why did you put us up? Do you belong to the Salvation Army?' See Simone Pétrement *Simone Weil*, trans. Raymond Rosenthal (Mowbrays, London and Oxford 1977), p. 188.

[2] See on the biological views of Michurin and Lysenko, C. D. Darlington's *Genetics and Man*, pp. 211 ff.

As for the rest, one has to give in to the state as a necessity, but not accept it within oneself. It is often very difficult to do this, especially if one has been brought up in a certain atmosphere. One has to refuse to recognise rewards (one can, fortunately, refuse rewards if not punishments), and make the greatest use possible of the freedom we are allowed by the state (it seldom happens that citizens dare to make use of all the rights they have).

One also has the duty, contrary to the law, to take liberties which the state does not allow us, as long as such action is worth the trouble. It is a duty, if circumstances allow it, to choose the least evil among a number of forms of government. The least evil state is the one in which one is least dragooned by the state, where the ordinary citizens have more power to control things (decentralisation); state affairs are publicly known, and not kept secret; the mass of people are educated.

There is a duty to work for a change in the way society is organised: to increase the material welfare and technical and theoretical education of the masses.

International relations (the foreign policy of the state)

Diplomacy

Diplomacy is something secret. There is no way of controlling it. Diplomacy has to do with the whole life of the citizens. So an irresponsible state apparatus controls the life of the citizens without their knowing it. (Example: the secret clause of the treaty between France and Russia.[1])

The press plays a big part in all this. If there are papers one cannot corrupt, one can take them over. The press is the most powerful instrument of foreign policy. Spinoza[2]: 'It is better that

---

[1]   The treaty between France and Russia may refer to the Franco-Russian Treaty of 1897, which was secretly modified in 1899.

[2]   Spinoza's *Tractatus-Politicus*, chapter 7, section 28–29. The quotation is not accurate. Spinoza wrote: 'That dominion is most durable of all . . . which strives most eagerly by every means to avoid war and preserve peace. But I also admit that the counsels of such a dominion can hardly be concealed. But everyone will admit with me that it is far better for the right counsels of a dominion to be known to its enemies, than for the evil secrets of tyrants to be concealed from the citizens. They who

the state should have good plans known to its enemies, than bad ones hidden from its citizens. Those who can secretly rule over the affairs of the state have it completely in their power; just as they set traps for the enemy in time of war, so they do for the citizens in time of peace.'

In 1917, peace was rejected without the French people ever knowing that negotiations had taken place. Look at Paul Allard's[1] book about the committees that were held in secret. The speeches of Doumerge, Painlevé, Poincaré,[2] etc. are reproduced there, and no one has ever contradicted them. Poincaré kept in office and approved of Nivelle although everyone knew that he was not qualified. After the offensive at the Chemin des Dames[3] there were mutinies which were only to be expected; they were followed by executions after summary sentences. The officers chose the soldiers to be executed arbitrarily (they were generally the bravest). Pressure was brought on the war councils to force them to condemn what had happened. As for the chief culprits, nothing

can treat secretly of the affairs of a dominion have it absolutely under their authority, and, as they plot against the enemy in time of war, so do they against the citizens in time of peace. Now that this secrecy is often serviceable to a dominion no one will deny; but that without it the said dominion can subsist, no one will ever prove. . . . But the perpetual refrain of those who lust after absolute dominion is, that, it is to the essential interest of the commonwealth that its business be secretly transacted, and other like pretences, which end in the more hateful a slavery, the more they are clothed with a show of utility.' Spinoza, *Tractatus-Politicus*, trans. R. H. M. Elwes (Routledge & Sons, London 1895).

[1] Paul Allard, *Les Dessous de la guerre revélés par les comités secrets* (Editions de France, Paris 1932).

[2] Gaston Doumerge (1863–1937), French politician, President of the French Republic 1924–31; Paul Painlevé (1863–1933), French politician; Raymond Poincaré (1860–1934), French politician, President of the French Republic 1913–20. Cousin of Henri Poincaré (see p. 86, note 1).

[3] Chemin des Dames, where there was a French offensive against the Germans in 1917 led by General Nivelle who succeeded Marshal Joffre as General-in-Chief of the French army in 1916. After the unsuccessful offensive he was replaced by Marshal Pétain who, in 1940, arranged the armistice with the Germans and became head of the Vichy government. After the war Pétain was condemned to death in 1945, but the sentence was commuted to life imprisonment on the island of Yeu, where he died in 1951.

more was done than to relieve them of their commands. Everything went on in secret. All decisions which involve human lives are taken by people who have nothing to lose. As for the politicians, they had less to lose than the generals.

Are there any remedies? Those that have to do with the external relationships between states are illusory. There is no more control with the League of Nations[1] than without it. As long as there are states which cannot be controlled, all that kind of thing will be in vain.

The struggle for a good foreign policy is in fact the struggle for a good internal one. The more dependent the state feels itself, the more chances there are of avoiding disaster.

As long as diplomacy is something secret, it will be impossible, for the time being, to distinguish between offensive and defensive wars. The citizens will always be able to say: 'This war has been forced on us', but is it the government of their own country or that of the enemy country which has forced it on them? Those in power in each country respect each other.

It is the same people who believe that the Kellogg Pact [2] guarantees peace and that members of parliament represent the people! These are very simple, but quite naive beliefs.

Colonisation

This problem is identical with that of capitalism. Colonisation goes on to make big business even bigger, not for the benefit of the people colonised. To say: 'Colonisation must be reformed' is the same thing as saying: 'The social order must be transformed'. One has to see men and not things.

We can sum up the problem of colonisation in the following way:

Benefits: roads, railways, hospitals, schools, the destruction of

---

[1] The League of Nations was an organisation established for international co-operation at the initiative of the victorious Allied powers at the end of World War I with the aim of guaranteeing peace and security. It was replaced by the United Nations Organisation in 1946.

[2] The Kellogg-Briand Pact of 27 August 1928 outlawed war and provided for pacific settlement of disputes and was signed by sixty-five states in Paris.

superstitions and family oppression (the yoke borne by woman, etc.).

Disadvantages and horrors: see the articles in the *Petit Parisien*[1] published by Louis Roubard.[2] Corporal punishment, massacres, bombings; it does not matter at all to the French people that a foreman can, without being punished, murder a native in cold blood. Stories from Madagascar: the prisons are so full that there is no room in them for people who have been sentenced; so they have to have forced labour. See Gide[3]: the Congo, forced labour; it has been calculated that each metre of railway cost one human life, etc.

Conclusion: colonisation was often begun by very fine people: explorers, missionaries. Now everything is a matter of state policy. Things will always be the same as long as men are subordinated to things. Although there is a difference of degree, there is no difference in kind between what goes on in a country itself and what goes on in its colonies. All the same, there should be some attempt to make these horrors less with a little more human feeling.

Conclusion: the relations of the individual with society

The ideal in accordance with which society should be ordered is co-operation, that is to say exchange of labour. This is the only kind of relationship which agrees with Kant's formulation of the moral law: to treat human beings always as ends.

The division of labour has made each man just a cog in a

---

[1] *Petit Parisien* – a French daily newspaper which went out of circulation just before World War II.

[2] Louis Roubaud (1884–1941), French writer and journalist who wrote a number of books on the French colonies: *Vietnam, la tragedie indochinoise* (L. Valois, Paris 1931); *Mograb* (B. Grasset, Paris 1934); and with Gaston Pelletier: *Images et réalités coloniales* (A. Tourmon, Paris 1931), and *Empire ou colonies* (Plon, Paris 1936).

[3] André Gide (1869–1951), French novelist who won the Nobel prize in 1947. Perhaps his best known novel is *The Strait Gate*. His writings contain much criticism of what he thought of as generally accepted attitudes. See his *Travels in the Congo*, trans. D. Bussy (A. A. Knopf, New York and London 1930).

machine. One can no longer even say that slaves serve free men, because slaves in our society are only fodder for machines.

What can one do? One has to try to bring about conditions favourable to this ideal form of government by making it easy for the masses to be educated (and this must not be confused with state propaganda). One can submit to, but one cannot accept the way production is now organised. If one stops oneself from thinking of all this, one makes oneself an accomplice in what is happening. One has to do something quite different: take one's place in this system of things and do something about it.

4

Ethics and aesthetics

> 'If the world is divine, all is well;
> if the world is given over to chance,
> don't allow yourself to go the same way.'
> 'Thought, freed from passions, is a fortress.'
> (Marcus Aurelius)

Morals founded on something other than conscience

Morals based on interest

A. Eudaemonism.

Aristippus,[1] the Cyrenaic, who lived at the same time as Plato, a pupil of Socrates. (N.B. Socrates showed such freedom in his thought that his pupils went in all directions): the good is pleasure. Any kind of pleasure.

Epicurus[2] (fourth century) said: the good is pleasure which has been calculated; that means that it does not run the risk of being followed later by something bad. He distinguished between 'pleasure which comes from rest' and 'pleasure which comes from movement'. The first is nothing but the absence of pain; that means that the soul which is free from pain can find enjoyment in itself.

Pleasure which comes from rest is always pure; it means coming to that state in which the soul delights in its own existence. That amounts to a rule of life which is the same as that of the Stoics. (Cf. Spinoza: 'Bliss is not the reward of virtue, but virtue itself.'[3])

B. Utilitarianism.

Bentham[4]: the good is the interest of the greatest number.

---

[1] Aristippus, date uncertain, probably a little older than Plato.

[2] Epicurus (341–270 B.C.). The word 'Epicurean' gives no idea at all of his thought. Lucretius's *De rerum natura* derives its ideas from Epicurus, who was influenced by the fifth-century Greek philosopher, Democritus.

[3] Spinoza, *Ethics*, Bk V, Prop. XLII.

[4] Jeremy Bentham (1748–1832), English jurist and philosopher. See his 'An Introduction to the Principles of Morals and Legislation' in *The Works of Jeremy Bentham*, Vol. I (Russell & Russell, New York 1962).

One can always ask oneself, when dealing with a moral question, how a utilitarian would tackle the question. Example: punishment is something bad because it harms the culprit; it is good because it prevents crimes. One simply makes an arithmetical calculation.

Examination of this view: pleasure is, by definition, an end in itself, but the pleasure of one's neighbour is not an end in itself. Once it is a question of my neighbour's pleasure, it is no longer an end for me.

That is just a philosophical fraud.

It would then be a matter of establishing a relationship between my own pleasure and my neighbour's, between an individual interest and the general interest.

Tyrants always appeal to the general interest, it is always possible for them to prove that it is a bad thing to upset the social order.

People in the eighteenth century made the mistake of believing that society is a sum of individuals.

While in the nineteenth century, people saw that it was rather a relationship between individuals, and that the general interest depended on social structure.

Note that all unsuccessful acts of aggression are thought to be crimes, while those which have been successful are later praised. In social conflicts, those who are defeated are damned. That is quite natural, because they appear to be bringing destruction and not construction.

Tyrants are not hypocrites in appealing to the general interest.

Oppression is found when the social structure and individuals are opposed to one another. The general interest is the interest of those who have the social machine under their control, and is opposed to the interest of those who are subject to them.

All movements of liberation have been the work of individuals. This is a good way of finding out whether there is oppression: see whether an appeal is made to the general interest.

Cf. Rousseau's[1] remark on what Caiaphas said: 'Oportet unum hominem pro populo mori.' (It is necessary for one man to die on the people's behalf.)

[1] See Rousseau, *The Social Contract*, Bk IV, chapter 8.

The lives of the majority of people are under the control of a few individuals. This view then ends up by being self-contradictory.

In fact, Bentham was led to speak of the universal interest of individuals, when he spoke of the general interest. One can, in fact think of individuals in two ways. The interest of an individual thought of as a human being, disregarding contingencies, leads us on to a morality of conscience. That is what happened to Bentham without his realising it.

Bentham did not see what the problem was: what is more, at one time he emphasised one side of the question, and then the other; he did not see how ambiguous the general interest is. His morality was conservative in its foundations, although he did not realise this, while he himself was a radical (he belonged to the extreme left of that time).

Morality based on instinct

The British school: Hume, Adam Smith.[1]

Adam Smith put forward a clear idea of political economy. He was the forerunner of economists of the nineteenth century. His views are very important.

This morality based on instinct depends on a simple idea: when others suffer, we suffer too.

Examination of this theory: it ignores matters of conscience and inner conflicts. Virtue is not involved if one helps someone else with the aim of doing oneself a good turn.

The Stoics said that virtue is a weakness. Let us take some examples. Jean Valjean,[2] in *Les Misérables* (the case of the brainstorm) is very fine: what was it that made Jean Valjean give himself up? He did not know the old gentleman, but he did know that he was good for nothing; on the other hand he was responsible for his fellow workers; every feeling of solidarity and sympathy should have made him keep quiet. (One might say that Jean

[1] Adam Smith (1723–90), Scottish economist, whose *Wealth of Nations* put forward *laissez-faire* economics.
[2] Jean Valjean, one of the characters in Victor Hugo's *Les Misérables*, trans. I. F. Hapgood (Collins, London and Glasgow 1955).

Valjean was not a real person. Yes, but our admiration for him is quite real.)

There is certainly no solidarity nor sympathy in all those instances where one does harm to one's neighbours, and good to people far away. We all live by treading on human beings, but we do not give it a thought; it takes a special effort to remember them. When we make a rare and praiseworthy effort to direct our attention to things which we easily forget, this is to be explained by our desire to be sincere with ourselves; it is not to be explained by sympathy, since an effort of this kind results in suffering.

All those who break with their surroundings in order to be faithful to what they think cause pain to others and to themselves. Examples: Francis of Assisi; the Christian martyrs of pagan families; nowadays conscientious objectors.

No material good is achieved if one speaks the truth about public affairs: one only increases the evil one wants to check, because people react to this by expressing quite different opinions etc.

So there is something else apart from the 'morality based on instinct'.

Guyau[1] called his morality 'morality without obligation or sanction'.

Comment: sanctions have nothing to do with morality, but one has to feel an obligation if one is to practise virtue.

There is something within us which constrains us with the force of an imperative. When one is virtuous, one has the impression that one does the opposite of what one would naturally do.

Sociological moralities

Durkheim, Lévy-Bruhl.

They say: when one is virtuous, one has the feeling that one obeys a higher power; the command is issued by society. It is something external, because we are dominated by society; it is internal because we have the thoughts of society within us. If we consider morality to be something transcendent, it is for this reason.

[1] Marie-Jean Guyau (1854–88), French philosopher. See *A Sketch of Morality Independent of Obligation or Sanction*, trans. G. Kapteyn (Watts & Co., London 1898).

The proofs they give are:

1. The resemblances there are between the different moralities of the same period, whatever the foundations are. (Example: the Stoics and Epicureans.)

2. The differences between the moralities of different periods.

Examination of this sociological morality
Evolution of morality:

In the family (incest, female chastity, marriages of children in India, etc.).

Family morality changes with the structure of society. (It is because of social attitude that adultery is considered to be more serious in a woman than a man.)

At the level of duties between different kinds of men:

For example: to kill a slave was not a shameful thing to do in Rome. Even in Seneca we find that he praises the magnanimity of the master who was not cruel towards his slaves, as if that ought not to be taken for granted. In the Middle Ages – the feudal system; everything depended on the master's word.

Today, everything depends on questions of money. Speculation was at other times thought to be dishonest; nowadays the only place to win a fortune is the Stock Exchange. There is no longer any relationship between a fortune and work. Swindling has penetrated everywhere; advertising is always a bluff and no one can do without it and competition forces one to employ the same swindling methods as the next man.

One sees changes in morality also taking place within the same period.

For example, during the war, everything was turned upside down; human relationships were changed, all relationships based on collaboration were destroyed except for those brought about by high finance. During the war, German science and culture were destroyed (what Barrés, Bazin said etc., glorifying the grandeur of war, its purifying and divine quality).

The same things happen in civil wars (the Commune of 1871).

During the floods of 1910 it was quite normal for people to give shelter to people they found driven out on the road, whereas now one would be thought a bit mad if one gave shelter to a vagabond.

The very feelings which it was necessary to tone down if one exhibited them in 1789, had to be exaggerated in 1792 to make any impression at all.

After these considerations and examples, we can ask ourselves: 'What is it, in morality, that depends on social relationships?' The commonly held and current view of morality: one might say that the more civilised a society is the less disagreement there is between its social morality and true morality.

A highly civilised society would be one in which one could be perfectly and conscientiously virtuous, think seriously about everything one did, and not be insulted.

The conception of honour too changes with circumstances. Honour is something which is intermediate between the vulgar social morality and the true morality. Honour exists at different levels. The judgement of society which is called forth independently of the presence of society can be called honour. The judgement of public opinion is so powerful that we cannot prevent ourselves from taking it into account. Honour can become identical with pure virtue if it is taken to a limit: if instead of saying: 'What would public opinion think of me? one says 'What would a sensible man say about me?' The sensible man is then no different from our own conscience.

It is respect for the dead that above all brings about this change.

Theological morality: God (or the gods)

Religion too lays down ends (as the morality of pleasure, and that of the general interest do). It imposes taboos: one must not do a certain thing because it is forbidden by the gods. There are commands which are purely religious. These commands change a great deal as time goes on, just as social commands do.

One can cite: religious murders in human sacrifices and in some wars (wars in ancient times, 'wars of religion', Inquisition, etc.), religion establishing castes (in India).

All rites have their origin in religious commands, and by, definition, the commands change as the religion itself does. A religion which is intolerant commands its members to fight those who do not belong to it.

The more pure a religion is, the more its commands resemble moral commands.

It is often tempting to explain moral commands by religion. For example, what do you tell a child if you want to explain to him that he should not tell lies? If the family is a religious one one will explain to the child that God knows everything. This answer to the child's question makes a policeman of God. Obedience which is understood in this way is not a virtue.

Socrates[1]: 'Will you say that a pious man is pious because the gods approve of him, or is it that the gods approve of him because he is pious?'

So, if God is someone external to oneself he is a God like a commissioner of police; and if he is someone within oneself, he does not provide any solution to the problem of morality.

It is rather the moral ideal which proves God, and not God who proves the moral law.

God cannot solve the problem of morality.

Kant: 'If one could verify or prove God, the law would never be broken.'

Those who believe that they can come into contact with God through experience (mystical) are guilty of blasphemy. In this way the divine is destroyed.

By definition, in so far as he is the highest value, God is indemonstrable. God cannot be felt. 'Truly, thou art a hidden God.'[2] One can say that the very reason why God has decided to

---

[1] See Plato's *Euthyphro*, p. 12C. The translation of this passage of Plato is not correct in the notes. It should be: 'Is what is holy, holy, because it is loved by the gods, or is what is holy loved by the gods because it is holy?' The incorrect translation seems to accord with the ideas expressed in this section on 'theological morality'. Though they are views which Simone Weil did not hold at the end of her life. See her letters to Father Perrin in *Waiting on God*.

[2] 'Truly thou art a hidden God.' Simone Weil quotes Isaiah 45.15 from the Vulgate translation of the Old Testament. The complete verse is: 'Vere tu es Deus absconditus, Deus Israel salvator' (Truly thou art a hidden God, thou God of Israel, the saviour). Simone Weil frequently in her writings inveighs against the God of the Old Testament, the God

hide himself is that we might have an idea of what he is like. Every attempt to base morality on theology destroys both morality and theology. One shouldn't say: 'I have to do this because it is God's will', but: 'God wills it because I have to do it.' In that case God simply gives one the strength to do it.

The change from the Old Testament to the New marks the change from the God who is outside to the God who is within.

Claudel: 'What is there that is weaker and less powerful than God, since he can do nothing without us?'[1]

of Israel, and the section called 'Israel' in the French edition of *Gravity and Grace* was not included in the English translation. The Hebrew original does seem to mean rather: 'Truly thou art a God who hides himself' (rather than 'hidden God'). Simone Weil is reported here to have said that God does hide himself, and the note continues: 'One can say that the very reason why God has decided to hide himself is that we might have an idea of what he is like.' (It might seem more reasonable to say that God hides himself so that we might have no idea of what he is like. See Exodus 33.22–3, where God says to Moses: 'You must stand in the rock, and when my glory passes by, I will put you in a cleft of the rock and shield you with my hand while I pass by. Then I will take my hand away and you shall see the back of me; but my face is not to be seen.') What Simone Weil wrote later about this is very different from what we find in these notes. See, for example, *Gravity and Grace*, p. 103: 'A case of contradictories which are true. God exists: God does not exist. Where is the problem? I am quite sure that there is a God in the sense that I am quite sure my love is not illusory. I am quite sure that there is not a God in the sense that I am quite sure nothing real can be anything like what I am able to conceive when I pronounce the word. But that which I cannot conceive is not an illusion.' That raises the question of whether anyone *does* understand what is said about Yahweh in the Old Testament.

[1] Paul Claudel (1868–1955), French poet and playwright. The quoted sentence comes from his play *The Hostage*. But it is misquoted. What Claudel wrote was: 'Quoi de plus faible et de plus desarmé que Dieu, quand Il ne peut rien sans nous.' (What is there that is weaker and more defenceless than God, since he can do nothing without us.) The notes, however, have: 'Quoi de plus faible et de plus impuissant que Dieu, puisqu'Il ne peut rien sans nous.' The words are spoken in the play (act II, scene ii) by a priest, Monsieur Badillon who is trying to persuade Sygne that it is her duty to marry Baron Turelure (whom she does not want to marry) because the Baron is able to spare the life of the Pope and that of Georges. Sygne says to Badillon: 'Let God do his own duty as I do mine.' Then Badillon says: 'What is there that is weaker...' See English translation by Pierre Chavannes (Oxford University Press, London 1917).

The true foundations of morality

Kant and the categorical imperative

'Do what you should, come what may.' This is a categorical imperative, not a hypothetical one.

(Cf. Kant. While hypothetical imperatives have to do with means, categorical imperatives have to do with ends, ends of such a sort that consequences do not matter.)

What is the source from which we get the categorical imperative?

It is impossible to prove virtue. One might say that the proof's proof is virtue itself.

Every time one gives a proof, one only proves the part the mind plays. Proofs depend on hypotheses which in turn depend on the part played by thought, which is by definition indemonstrable.

Kant[1]: 'Act only according to that maxim which you can at the same time will to become a universal law.' 'Act as if the maxim of your action were to become through your action a universal law of nature.' (To put it another way, one sees things from God's point of view.)

Example of suicide when one is in despair; it is impossible to think of the destruction of everything. In the case of other people we want their faculties to be improved, so, we want the same thing for ourselves. There are two kinds of sin: those which have to do with a maxim that becomes contradictory if it is thought of as universal (examples: false promises, suicide, etc.); and those which have to do with a maxim which is not contradictory, but which no one could will universally. One can really be fully conscious only in so far as one is virtuous.

But what Kant said is quite negative; it eliminates some things, but it does not give us any end; one has to look for the highest end of all, an end which can be universal for all human beings.

For a reasonable being, there can only be one end: reason itself. A reasonable being is an end in himself in so far as he is a being who thinks. To sacrifice oneself as a thinking being is the destruction of virtue.

[1] Kant, *Groundwork of the Metaphysics of Morals*, trans. H. J. Paton (Hutchinsons's University Library, London 1947), chapter 2.

Kant: 'Act only in such a way that you treat humanity, whether in respect of your own person or in respect of anyone else, always as an end, and never as a means.'

For example, it is not forbidden to allow men to work for us, but we should treat these workers as thinking beings. Every time you speak to someone who serves you only as someone who is your servant, you think of him only as a means. Kant's formula is like what we find in the Gospel: 'Love your neighbour as yourself.'

Duties towards oneself: to subordinate everything to this highest of ends: thinking. Even if one were alone in the world, there would be a reason for living.

Duties towards others: this is a mirror image of one's duties towards oneself.

The best known kind of devotion (of an old servant to her mistress, a wife to her husband, etc.) is a failure in virtue; the devotion in these cases is to the material welfare of the other person rather than to his nobility of character. Once one understands that all there is to respect in another person is 'virtue', one cannot respect anyone else more than oneself; if one did one would be renouncing perfection. 'Be ye perfect as your heavenly father is perfect.'[1] Perfection is a duty. It is impossible to love a man because he is superior; if one loves perfection, one loves it for itself; so, one does not love it more in others than in oneself.

Social duties: in so far as social relationships overlap with one's relationships with individuals, and, as far as it is possible, one must look to see how one can lessen, in society, those things which bring about oppression.

Conclusion: the moral end is to do nothing which sullies human dignity, in oneself or in another. One cannot set out to save souls; to begin with that is pride with a vengeance; all one can do is to remove for others the things which prevent them from understanding things clearly. All that is purely negative. The problem is not one of trying to do good, but of trying to avoid evil. One can never say one is generous, because, whenever one helps people in distress, one is only redeeming oneself to a very small degree.

[1] St Matthew 5.48.

The rational moralists
Socrates

The first person who followed a morality based on reason was Socrates. Socrates said that 'No man is voluntarily wicked', that one is wicked through ignorance of the good, that furthermore, the good is neither pleasure nor power and that one cannot be master of anything, whatever it is, unless one is first master of oneself. He used to say that the good is to keep one's soul free from all impurity, from all attacks of passion. Evil is always a weakness, and virtue is always strength, even if things appear to be quite the opposite (a tyrant, and men tortured by a tyrant). A tyrant is, although he does not know it, weaker than the person who, fully aware of what is happening, allows himself to be killed by tyrants. Socrates, if we can believe Plato's dialogues, used to set forth his ideas in myths. The highest principle is clearly: 'Know yourself', since evil is defined as self-ignorance.

The current view is that this morality is intellectualist in character. In fact, that is completely false: in a morality that is intellectualist, attempts are made to prove the good. (Bentham: good subordinated to a calculus.)

For Socrates, virtue and clear thoughts come from the same source, from the same power within, conscience.

Plato

He only developed the moral ideas of Socrates.

In the myth of the cave,[1] Plato has made explicit the relationship between virtue and thought, which was implicit with Socrates.

Intellectual training (mathematics) is indispensable if one is going to find the source of virtue. As long as one has not reached mind, which is the source of both thought and virtue, truth has no sense, thoughts have no value. (N.B. One has to go beyond the sciences to contemplate the activity of mind itself.) Moral salvation and intellectual salvation are one and the same; one has to withdraw one's soul from what passes in order to direct it to what

[1] Plato, *Republic*, Bk. VII.

is, that is to say one has to deliver it from the passions. If one is not trained to think, free of the influence of the passions, by means of pure reason, one cannot achieve this. Intelligence depends on virtue, and virtue on intelligence.

Plato[1] distinguishes between three parts in a man: mind, passion, desires. The metaphor of the sieve: a covering which contains a small man; reason: a huge lion; passion: a hydra with many heads, some of which are fierce (insatiable desires: vices), others of a gentler kind (normal desires: hunger, thirst, etc.). What is needed is an internal harmony. Justice consists of satisfying the lion and the hydra only as far as it does not impede reason. The wise man should use his passion to tame his desires.

One must bring oneself into harmony with pleasures that are pure. It is easy to distinguish them: the insatiable pleasures are impure (the passion of the drug addict, the gambler, the drunkard). Examples of pure pleasures: sport without championships; eating and drinking sparingly when one has worked well; the pleasures of friendship (Montaigne and La Boétie[2]). The wise man is the only person who knows what true pleasure is.

The Cynic morality

It derives from that of Plato.

Antisthenes[3] is the first of the Cynics. (He is mentioned in the *Phaedo*.)

Diogenes[4] is the most famous. His reply to Alexander is well known: 'Get out of my light.'

If one does good to someone, one has one judge less. That is the greatest power of the tyrant. Diogenes knew how to scorn good turns. One of Diogenes's maxims was 'It is pain that is good' (not the pain one has to suffer, but the pain which is voluntary).

[1] Plato, *Republic*, Bk. IV and *Gorgias*, 493Bff.
[2] Montaigne (1533–92) and La Boétie (1530–63), both French writers, were close friends.
[3] Antisthenes (444–365 B.C.), Greek philosopher, a disciple of Socrates. See Diogenes Laertius, *Lives of the Philosophers*, Bk VI.
[4] Diogenes (413–327 B.C.), Greek philosopher. The story referred to here is that when Alexander the Great asked Diogenes whether there was anything he wanted, he got the reply: 'Get out of my light.'

His ideal was to be detached from everything: he broke his mug in pieces and used his hand to drink. His independence was complete: to desire nothing in order to be independent.

The Stoics

They are the direct descendants of the Cynics. Zeno, Cleanthes, Chrysippus are the three successive heads of the Greek Stoic school. In Rome there were Seneca, Epictetus, Marcus Aurelius[1] (but the last two wrote in Greek).

There is a Stoic physics, logic, philosophy.

Among them too, the relation between thought and morality was particularly emphasised.

For them, as long as a men had a mind unfettered, he lacked nothing in the world.

Epictetus: 'No one can take away free will.'

Marcus Aurelius: 'Thought freed from passion is a fortress.'

And so, all the paradoxes: 'Only the wise man is noble, free, etc.'

The only fault is to allow the passions to gain control of his fortress. When the Stoics said: 'All faults are the same', that meant that the significance of the fault depends on the circumstances of the moment, that, once one has lost control of oneself one can do anything which the circumstances favour. One cannot lose one's self control by degrees so that it is at one time greater than at another; one simply loses it for a longer or shorter time. In the eyes of the Stoics, once reason lost control to passion, nothing is better than anything else.

Goethe[2] said: 'I have never heard any crime mentioned which I did not feel capable of committing.'

There is no break in continuity between some vague idea of a possible crime and the act of committing it.

There are two rules which we must follow:

(a) to prevent oneself acting on the first impulse;

---

[1] Zeno (355–263 B.C.), Cleanthes (333–232 B.C.), Chrysippus (280–207 B.C.), Epictetus (55–135 B.C.), Seneca (4 B.C.–A.D. 65), Marcus Aurelius (121–180).

[2] Goethe, *Maxims and Reflections*, no. 240. 'Man darf nur alt werden, um milder zu sein; ich sehe keinen Fehler, den ich nicht auch begangen hätte.'

(b) to surround oneself with external barriers in order to prevent passion from developing and give good sense time to intervene.

One should not wish for arbitrary power, to be in a position which enables one to make an attempt on someone else's life (and that can be done by words just as easily as with a revolver).

Every failure is lack of self-control. As long as one has control of oneself nothing evil can take place. In order to reach this stage, the Stoics put forward a complete theory of judgement. For example, to resist seduction, say to yourself: 'These fair voices are only disturbances in the air; these fine fabrics are only vegetable, etc.' In the same vein: suffering is only suffering, because we think of it in that way. All likes and dislikes have their roots in judgement; but, if we want to, we can always control our judgements.

Marcus Aurelius said: 'The soul is untouched by things; they are completely external to it', and again: 'Things do not come to you, it is you who go towards things. Things have no way of access into the soul, and cannot move the soul; the soul moves itself.'

The natural outcome of the idea that man can always be free is Stoic optimism; ancient stoicism was a universal love for everything, not the so called 'stoic resignation' as is commonly said today. The world is our country because it allows us to live as men, always; we are its citizens.

Marcus Aurelius: 'Everything is in harmony with me. I am in harmony with everything, for I am in harmony with you, O world! Nothing happens too early or too late for me since everything happens at its proper time for you. O world of nature, everything which your seasons bring is fruit for me. Everything comes from you, everything exists in you, everything has you as its end. Someone else said: "O beloved city of Cecrops!" (Athens), and I, why should I not say: "O beloved city of Zeus!" (the universe).' 'Not to accept everything which happens with this holy love, is to cut oneself off from the city, to become a stranger in the world.' 'He who renounces the world's reason and suffers what happens to him resentfully, is an abscess on the world, for nature which brought you that, also brought you yourself into existence.'

There is but one nature which is the origin of everything; if you accept your own existence, you ought to accept everything, because: 'The universe is harmed if one breaks into its chain of causes. Now you break this chain, although it is part of you, if you are dissatisfied with anything which happens.' 'Everything is equally bad if it makes you lose your self-control; everything is equally good if it leads to action and being a man.'

Rule about suffering: 'This cucumber is bitter, throw it away; there are brambles in your way, avoid them; that is enough.' Do not add: 'Why are these things to be found in the universe?'

The religious view of the Stoics: it is pantheistic; for them the world is divine. They thought of the gods and men as fellow citizens. If a man is wise, he is the equal of the gods, because there are not two reasons; there is only one single reason. Men and the gods communicate with each other through the world; the world is the city of beings endowed with reason; it is divine in so far as it allows divine beings (men and gods) to live in it. The religion of the Stoics is this relationship between the world and man; one is reasonable in so far as one loves the world.

So: no resignation, but joy. Pity and feelings like it are banned. One should accept all suffering with joy (those for which one is not responsible, of course). St Francis of Assisi was a perfect Stoic, Descartes was to some extent, and so was Goethe to a very high degree. Rousseau and Kant were a little. Of course, Stoicism makes itself particularly felt when it is expressed in poetry. That is why Francis of Assisi and Goethe are the best examples.

Let us think of pantheism in connection with the Stoics. The question arises in connection with the opposition there is between a transcendent God (who is beyond our grasp) and an immanent God. Plato thought of God as transcendent. The question is one which is related to the ideas one has of the relationships between the mind and the body. One thinks that there is a relationship of harmony between the mind and the body just as one thinks that there is one between God and the world.

Now, we have to think of matter both as an obstacle and as a means.

Kant: 'The light-winged dove, when in its free flight it beats the air and feels its resistance, might well believe that it would fly even better in a void.'

So, we have to struggle against the world as a swimmer does against the water, as the dove struggles against the air, but we have to love it as the swimmer loves the water that bears him up, etc. The Stoics brought these two feelings together and it is the second which seems more important – that of the love of the world.

So pantheism follows naturally from a way of thinking of the relationships of the soul and the body, of the relationships between theory and practice.

Descartes

For him, pure reason (mathematical deduction) plays the same role as it does in Plato. The original sin is error, virtue is freedom, as it was for Socrates, Plato, Diogenes, the Stoics.

'I believe that the true generosity which enables a man to think as highly of himself as he legitimately can consists only in part in his knowing that there is nothing which really concerns him except the free control of his will, and that the only reason why he should be praised or blamed is because he has made good or bad use of it, and also in his feeling within himself a firm and determined resolve to make good use of it – that is to say never to fail in his determination to plan and do those things which he will judge to be the best; and this is to follow virtue perfectly.'

The soul is one and does not contain divisions. The soul must succeed in bending the body itself to reason. That might appear to be paradoxical, but it can happen because thought is exercised with movement and because one can make this training a matter of practice (see the *Treatise on the Passions*). 'With a little effort, one can have an influence on the brains of animals, so one can do it even more in the case of a man who can reason.' The lever one has to use is: the conditioned reflex. Punishment is only an attempt to bring into existence painful associations.

We have to think of our bodies as something which we conquer by systematic action.

Descartes dealt at some length with the consequences of his moral view.

In principle everyone is equal.

One must treat everyone as one's equal.

The mind can draw directly on a certain strength from the body; still the passions are stronger. But it is possible to overcome them by careful thought. (Cf. 'Man controls nature by obeying.') Everyone has it in their power to have complete control over their passions.

To sum up:

1. Duty towards oneself is to be free, that means: (a) to rescue the mind from being overcome by the body; (b) to put the body under the control of mind.

2. Duty towards others is to think of all men as one's equals. What is original in Descartes, is the idea that everyone can know the truth, so that there is a duty to instruct everyone if one can. Descartes made his servants mathematicians; one of them, after he left Descartes' service, went to a Dutch university, as teacher of mathematics.

Descartes' religion: we have no knowledge of ourselves except in relation to God; we know God before we know ourselves. Descartes said that there is nothing like knowing the truth in God's case, because it is because God wills it that two and two make four; that there is nothing like necessity in God, otherwise there would no longer be any activity in God, and God would be even inferior to man. He would be no more than a machine that thinks, Descartes attributes to God only pure judgement, that is to say pure will.

God is beyond ideas just as Plato's Good is. The view that Descartes had of God was of a God who is completely transcendent, whom one does not meet in the world, which is pure matter. (Descartes insisted much more on the opposition between God and the world, as he did on that between mind and body, than he did on their union.) Descartes was a man of action, while the Stoics and St Francis of Assisi were much more contemplative by nature.

Rousseau

He holds to the same relation between virtue and thought. He thinks that will and judgement have the same source: 'If someone asks me for the cause which determines my will, I, in turn, ask what is the cause which determines my judgement, for it is clear that these two causes are one and the same and if one has a clear understanding that man is active in his judgements, that his understanding is only the power he has to make comparisons and judgements, one will see that his freedom is only a power of the same kind or derived from it; he chooses the good in the same way as he judges what is true; if his judgement is bad, so is the choice he makes...'

Duty towards oneself: freedom.

Duty towards others: equality.

The 'social contract' is a search for an ideal society. In the eighteenth century many people believed that society had its origin in a contract: Rousseau did not hold this.

But a just society would be one where men would be bound together by a free and mutual consent. Equality has its origin in freedom: once one has power over the unlimited faculty of freedom, everyone is equal. So social equality is not the negation of natural inequalities, but those beings who, in so far as they are things are unequal, are equal in so far as they are minds.

So, the first thing to be sought is freedom.

Kant

The categorical imperative, as we have already seen, is defined by its being universal. Duty is to consider what is human as the highest end.

Kant's religious views:

Here below, it is impossible to treat men otherwise than as if they were things, means. For example, in the poet Sully Prudhomme[1]: 'No one can boast that he has no use for men.' Sully Prudhomme loved the baker because he made bread, the mason

---

[1] Sully Prudhomme (1839–1907), French poet, winner of the Nobel Prize 1901. See his poem 'La justice'. The line quoted here comes from his poem 'Un songe' (A Dream) l. 13, in his work *Stances et poèmes.*

> Je connus mon bonheur et qu'au monde où nous sommes
> Nul ne peut se vanter de se passer des hommes;
> Et depuis ce jour-là je les ai tous aimés.

> I learnt how to be happy in this world;
> For none can boast to have no use for men,
> And from that day each one became my friend.

because the mason is a means of building houses. This poetry teaches one, in fact, to despise men. In this base view of the world, the relationship between men is one of treating each other as means. We hope for an ideal society of reasonable beings where each reasonable being will be for each of the others as he is for himself. For Kant the 'I ought' applies to every reasonable being. Each person wills the moral law, decrees it even as God does, in the realm of ends. So far, God is then only the idea of a free and perfect being.

If the question of God's existence is raised, it has to do with the relationships between this world and the world of ends. One could say: 'The relationships that exist between men should be spiritual ones, not just something material.' But this is impossible, because man's physical nature is stronger than his spiritual nature at those times when it makes its needs felt. For example, if we had had nothing to eat for a few days and were to meet Socrates, we would think of him above all as a means. So, material relationships between things exist of necessity. But can there exist at the same time relationships of ends? This is a moral problem when it has to do with relations with oneself, and a social one if it has to do with the relationships that exist between men at large.

Could Sully Prudhomme love the baker who brought him bread as an end? It looks as if that is impossible. One would be tempted to reject the idea outright, but where morality is concerned it is a matter of duty, not possibilities. Kant: 'You ought, therefore you can.'[1] Belief in the existence of God meant for Kant that there was no incompatibility between the world of means and that of ends. It is this kinship which one is referring to by the term 'God'. One cannot prove God: one would destroy him if one did that.

Belief in God becomes a duty. The honest man should say: 'I wish there were a God' (not 'I know'; that would be absurd). The virtuous man proves God by his virtue. It is not virtue which proceeds from God, but God who proceeds from virtue.

---

[1] Kant, *Critique of Practical Reason*, trans. T. K. Abbott (Longmans, Green, London 1901), pp. 106 ff. and 126 ff. and 'Preface to the Metaphysical Elements of Ethics' (in same translation), p. 290.

Belief in God is, for Kant, one of the three 'postulates of practical reason.'

The others are: freedom – and the belief in immortality, for if death is looked upon as a halt in the process of reaching perfection value is destroyed.

The relationship between the ideal and the real (God) is expressed by the moral sense.

The union between mind and body comes about through the moral sense.

God cannot be thought of as a union of soul and body, and for the same reasons.

The psychology of the aesthetic sense

'Beauty is the meeting place of the
mind with nature, where mind recognises
its good. There the true miracles, which
reconcile what is noble and base in man,
take place.' (Alain)[1]

The role of the body and of feeling

A. Behaviour: what is beautiful takes hold of the body. Ceremonies strongly influence our reactions (see Durkheim).

Dance: clearly it is something that is done.

Architecture: a child, as a matter of instinct, does not play around in a cathedral.

Music: all those who listen to it properly beat out the rhythm in some way or other. The rhythm and sound are two material elements.

Theatre: a play which does not move one is not a good one.

Poetry: what is fine about it disappears if, while keeping the sense the same, a few syllables are changed and the rhythm broken.

B. Further, there is a distinction between what is beautiful and what is pleasing.

1. Duration: one does not grow tired of beauty. One does grow tired of what is pleasing, of what only flatters the senses.

[1] Alain (Emile Chartier) (1868–1951), who taught Simone Weil philosophy at the Lycée Henri IV in Paris. See Simone Pétrement, *Simone Weil*, chapter 2.

2. Purity: beauty gives a pure pleasure – that is a pleasure which does not under any circumstances change into its opposite.

3. Infinity: one does not feel any change in one's appreciation in passing from one fine work to another, whatever these two works are. When we listen to a fugue by Bach, for example, if we think that there is some other piece which is finer, that is because we do not find truly beautiful the piece we are listening to at the moment. Beauty immediately suggests what is infinite.

4. No flattery: beautiful things make an immediate impact on our feelings (Romanesque churches; Homer, who is a finer poet than Vergil). Cf. Kant: 'Beauty is something which gives disinterested satisfaction.'

5. Universality: when one plays some fine piece of music, one feels one is enjoying it in the name of humanity as a whole.

It is pleasure felt as universal. Kant: 'Beauty has a universal appeal', or again, which comes to the same thing: 'Beauty is recognised as something which gives the satisfaction one needs.' One thinks that beauty is something inherent in the nature of beautiful things, whereas, when one smells a rose, one is well aware that the perfume is essentially a relationship between the object and ourselves.

Face to face with a work of beauty, on the other hand, we forget our own existence. We believe that works of art would keep all their value even if men no longer existed.

These are things of the mind.

Mind and understanding

A. Matter is subordinate to form: order, measure, proportion, regularity, hidden centres of symmetry (Gothic cathedrals).

Music: 'Music is a mathematics of the soul which counts without knowing it does' (Leibniz).

Transition of themes in music.

Poetry: rhythm.

This sort of kinship between beauty and the mind struck the Greeks very vividly (the Pythagoreans).

B. But:

1. Beauty is not a matter of instruction.

2. One does not surpass something beautiful; while one does go further than some idea or other.

There is no progression in what is beautiful, no order in the intellectual sense of the word, no relationship which can be isolated.

Kant expressed this by saying: 'The beautiful is a finality that has no end in view; and a universal satisfaction that does not depend on conceptual relationships.'[1]

There is no 'general idea' of aesthetic perfection: when one listens to a fugue by Bach, it is that that is perfect.

Harmony of body and mind in what is beautiful

Kant: 'Beauty is a harmony of the imagination and the understanding.'

The two things go together, there is a synthesis: beauty speaks at once to the intelligence, beauty is grasped immediately and intuitively by thought.

Now the essential difference is: reasoning is discursive, and intuitive thought is nothing but a feeling.

Generally where there is knowledge, appearances are given through the senses and one has to find out what lies behind them by reasoning. In the case of beauty, one grasps immediately what lies behind the appearances. (For example, a line of poetry which one has to scan in order to find out the number of feet is not a good line.) In architecture the relationships which make it what it is are grasped as they are by the senses; it is the same with rhythm in music.

Art for all its variety is always the same, an identity in variety.

Plato[2]: 'It seems to me that this tradition has been given men by the gods and has come upon us, with its very bright light, from heaven as the gift of some Prometheus; for it teaches us that all things are made of the one and the many, containing in themselves the limit and the unlimited.' 'All things are woven together from what is finite and what is not', that is to say: the knowledge of all

[1] Kant, *Critique of Judgement*, trans. J. H. Bernard, p. 45.
[2] Plato, *Philebus*, trans. with notes and commentary J. C. B. Gosling (Clarendon Press, Oxford 1975), p. 16c5.

things implies forms and numbers which have a well defined character and an indefinite variety. Nature, as man thinks of it, is a weaving together of the limited and the unlimited, and we have to grasp the indefinite variety by the limit. A continuous series enables us to grasp the infinite by what is limited (the series of natural numbers + 1).

This sameness in the variety brings about a harmony between mind and nature.

A cloudy sky where everything is continually changing is usually the kind of thing we have to understand rather than something regular (where each thing is subject to the influence of the whole). Furthermore, since we are placed at the point of view of our own intelligence and not at that of pure intelligence, we are not satisfied, because we are unable to grasp anything completely. On the other hand, in a starlit sky, one sees an object which the mind can grasp. One has the feeling of something eternal, of something pure, because the imagination cannot bring it within its scope. In a cloudy sky, we can imagine anything we wish. The simple relationships nature provides us with are of such great value because they seem to say to us: 'With your limited mind you can survive in the vastness of nature.' (Joy of the Pythagoreans in calling the world: κόσμος.) We feel a great joy when we are able to understand and still have command of our senses. In ordinary life we toss about among things about which we have no real thoughts because they are so familiar to us (a table) and those which make us feel dizzy. We try to get rid of what causes this giddiness by calculation, by using symbols that we can manage. Only, these symbols are not the world. We are perfectly happy when we can grasp the relationships apart from the symbols.

Beauty cannot be grasped by abstract concepts, and does not even let the imagination take hold of it. A Greek temple has a synthetic unity – that is to say it is something which brings together an infinite variety.

The unity of a work of art must be ceaselessly in peril and still be preserved at each instant.

Let us go over the different arts, the different areas of beauty.

Ceremony: if one were to replace living soldiers with wooden ones, there would no longer be any beauty. One has to have the impression that at each moment they are doing what they want, although they are not doing it.

Dance: at each moment passion is about to destroy the rhythm, but it never does.

Architecture: it creates an infinite number of appearances; it is a means of exploring space. In a temple, the succession of forms must be sufficiently unpredictable so that we feel the need to bring some feeling of unity into it. In a cathedral, each aspect begins by taking hold of our bodies in some particular way, and nevertheless, one knows that all these aspects have a complete unity about them: the form of the cathedral beneath which one is aware of an infinite number of relationships.

Music: (a) In its simplest form: song. The words change, and at each moment, it seems that the sound must change as the recital goes on, but, in fact, it doesn't change at all. (b) Instrumental music: one has to have the impression that it is the passion which brings a change in theme and which makes it come to an end. This is very noticeable in Beethoven: at times one says: 'That's the end, the passion has burst through', and then the theme returns.

Sculpture: cf. architecture; it is not an art on its own.

Painting: what makes it appeal to the mind is not the design; there must be harmony in the colours used.

Poetry: Phaedra's despair bursts forth into verse; and yet one has the impression at each moment that it is about to become nothing but shouts. The regularity has at each moment to be in jeopardy and yet win through. (This is very noticeable in Racine.)

Nature: there are times, when all at once, nature takes on the look of architecture. (We have to distinguish the beautiful from the sublime: a storm, a raging sea, are sublime.) One sees beauty in nature when it shows a regularity which is analogous to that which belongs to things that men have made. Nature must imitate art, and conversely, art must be as spontaneous as nature. What is beautiful should give one a feeling of familiarity, of belonging to one, and not the feeling of horror which one has when there is no form to distinguish (as is the case, for example, in a virgin forest). The element of familiarity comes from the relationships there are, from a geometrical element.

The human body: for it to be beautiful it must present a harmony, but the harmony should not be cold; it must be a harmony which is always at risk on account of movements, passions, and which, nevertheless, is preserved at each moment. This is very noticeable in sport.

Conclusion: the moral value of art

It teaches us that mind can come down into nature. Morality itself tells us to act according to thoughts that are true. Beauty is a witness that the ideal can become a reality.

5

Miscellaneous topics and essay plans

Self-knowledge
'Know thyself.' (Socrates)
'We only know what we appear to be.' (Kant)

Introduction:

A. One often speaks of the necessity of self-knowledge. But 'Know thyself' is ambiguous.

One must work out its different senses:

1. The ordinary senses are: (a) knowing oneself in order to change, to correct oneself. But that would be knowledge as a means, and Socrates was speaking of self-knowledge as an end; (b) knowing oneself in order to find out what one is capable of doing, to make good use of oneself; (c) knowing oneself in order to get to know human nature (Montaigne).

2. Besides this common way of thinking about it, 'Know thyself' was among the Greeks a precept which had become a proverb, and which was written up at the entrance to the temple at Delphi, which was a repository of all wisdom. What sense could this saying have had? It seems that it meant: 'Why do you have to come and ask me about the secrets of nature, of the future? All you need to do is know yourself.'

3. Now: Socrates had taken this saying as a motto. The imperative form 'Know thyself' shows very well that it is an end in itself, not a means. For Socrates, it is self-knowledge in opposition to knowledge about external things thought of as the ultimate end of all thought.

We leave out of account the senses which were mentioned first of all, and deal only with the last which is the most important to understand.

B. Why is this question interesting?

The knowledge of external things has no real interest, or, at least, is of less interest for men in general than self-knowledge. And, what is more, self-knowledge is the only thing that gives any value to any thought and action you care to think about.

C. But is it possible to know oneself and how?

We often think that we are mistaken about ourselves; self-knowledge in that case is not something that can be taken for granted. Some people have even thought that it is impossible, as Kant did when he said: 'We only know what is an appearance of ourselves.' End the introduction by pointing out that one has to give an answer to this question before it is possible to move on to any other.

I The search for the 'self'.

A. Begin with a few lines of a general character, referring to: character. It is the way in which other people judge us.

B. Introspection:

At first sight, it looks as if this reveals everything to us: the self and what is not the self. Let us find out what there is that belongs to the self in all this. Will? Intelligence? One cannot come to grips with them. Emotional states? They are something passive and one can only lay hold of those emotional states that have passed, which are therefore something which do not belong to us on two accounts.

Finish with a last paragraph on 'Time and the self'. What is there in common between the self of the present moment and the self of a year, a month, a day, an hour ago? (Examples of actual cases.) There is a fragment of the 'self' which continues to exist from one moment to the next. The term 'self' disappears, it has no sense. So the problem itself has none. We come to the conclusion of the first part: 'The self is a term which has no meaning.'

II Thought without the 'self'.

What is it we lose in doing away with the 'self'.

A. We lose our actions.

We can no longer refer to what we have already done. We are unable either to regret or be pleased about our actions, nor can we think of them as something we are sure about because things we have done many times in the past will become quite strange to us.

2. We cannot even think of directing our actions; our future actions do not belong to us. Now, all actions are a relationship between the present and the past. All human work is done with the future in view; the work always forms a bridge between the present and the future.

3. The very idea of action goes, for an action is something which goes on in time, a succession of attitudes co-ordinated in time. So, not only do our actions not belong to us, but they do not exist, they vanish at the same time as the 'self'.

B. We lose our thoughts.

1. We lose all the thoughts which are related to the 'self'.

2. This happens because all thoughts really have 'I' as subject.

Kant: 'It is only because I can grasp in a single consciousness different representations that I call them all *my* representations, for otherwise I would have a 'self' as varied and of as many colours as there are representations of which I am conscious.'

'The synthetic unity of consciousness is then an objective condition of all knowledge. Not only do I need it in order to know an object, but I have to refer every sensible intuition (sensation) to it for it to become an object for me.'

All thought implies a relationship, and it is always the 'I' which makes the relationship.

There would be no sense in saying 'The walls are grey' if they were grey for no one.

This is the turning point of the essay.

It is, in fact, the subject which has doubts of this kind about itself and this negation of all thought is one of its own thoughts.

III The 'I' and the 'self'.

The 'I' is not part of any feeling, of any action, etc. and nevertheless, every feeling, every action, etc. presupposes it. The pharisee confuses the 'I' with the 'self'; the sinner does not; repentance rises one above the level of action. So:

A. Everything that we actually know about ourselves is only appearance (actions – feelings – thoughts).

B. But that is already a negative form of knowledge of what we are (of the subject). And so the formula of Socrates has a sense. For him to distinguish between the 'I' and the 'self' would be the final end of all existence.

Let us see how this is so:

1. For thoughts: one can judge a thought only if one places it at a distance. Doubt means that the thinking subject is separated from his own thoughts which he can as a result examine. (If one confuses oneself with some thought one is lost.)

So, in the case of thoughts, 'Know yourself', means: 'Do not identify yourself with your thoughts.'

For example, a mathematician often loses himself in the theorems, formulae, etc. he is working on.

Science today often results in one's being deprived of consciousness.

2. With regard to feeling: one has to detach oneself from one's own feelings. The example of Turenne: 'You shiver, carcass...'[1]

What is said in the *Phaedo*: 'The soul holds conversations with its own desires, its own fears, its own feelings of anger, as if they did not belong to it.'

Forgiveness is an action in which one separates oneself off from one's own hate and spite.

3. In the field of action: to separate the 'I' from the 'self' in actions is to judge one's own actions, and never to become lost in the action.

One has to think about one's actions no longer in relation to oneself, but objectively.

Example: a thief thinks of stealing something as a means of making himself richer; his fault is that he only looks at the act in relationship to himself.

Conclusion:

In all circumstances, to be a man, is to know how to separate the 'I' and the 'self'. This is a task which never ends. Socrates

[1] Turenne – see p. 99, note 1.

reconciled Socrates and physics by using it to come to know himself.

> Illi mors mala incumbit
> Qui nimis notus omnibus
> Ignotus moritur sibi.[1]

> His death is something bad and vile
> When known the whole world o'er – he dies
> Unknown to none except himself.

The love of truth

Introduction:

An apparent paradox: one is presented with two ideas: 'love' and 'truth'.

Now 'love' is something which belongs to the emotions, and 'truth' to the mind.

The main difficulty here is: 'Something which belongs to the mind gives rise to feeling.'

I Obvious commonplaces.

All men love the truth.

The researches of scholars: Balthazar Claes in Balzac's[2] *The Quest for the Absolute*; Archimedes; explorers, investigators, etc.

II Passions which hide themselves under the love of truth: pride; vanity; a passion like that of a gambler (Claes), of a collector (historians); love of adventure (explorers) etc.

---

[1] These lines come from Seneca's play *Thyestes* (ll. 401–3). I have translated them as they appear in the notes, but they are not correctly quoted. Seneca wrote:

> Illi mors gravis incubat,
> Qui notus nimis omnibus,
> Ignotus sibi moritur.

Sir Thomas Wyatt (1503–42) translated them:

> For him death grippeth right hard by the crop
> That is much known of other, and of himself, alas,
> Doth die unknown, dazed, with dreadful face.

(The only alternative reading (of an ecclesiastical ms.) changes the 'illi' to 'nulli' and so completely negatives the sense.) See *The Ten Tragedies of Seneca*, trans. W. Bradshaw (Swan Sonnenschein & Co., 1902).

[2] Honoré de Balzac (1799–1850), French novelist whose work as a whole is usually referred to as *La Comédie Humaine*. See his *The Quest of the Absolute* (Everyman's Library, 1908).

The love of truth then is in itself very weak indeed. What is loved, is not the truth, but what gives pleasure; one believes that what is pleasing is true, and believes it sincerely.

The sources of the mistakes men make, is nothing but the weakness of their love of truth in relation to their other passions. III Still, we would not search for the truth at all if it were something that did not concern us. Search for the truth, of necessity, goes along with a love of a higher kind.

Where does this love come from? From all those feelings of a lower kind. The love of truth is the hatred of lying which the passions arouse by way of reaction once one has not blindly given oneself up to them.

Phaedra's reaction and feelings that she loved lying when she said: 'In misery I live and remember the sight of the holy sun, my ancestor.'[1] She dies with such love of purity that she is happy to purge the world of all the lies in her life.

Finally, relate this to the lives of real scientists (Archimedes); mathematics was for them the best thing to do in order to get some order into their thoughts.

Conclusion:

Truth is a means of purification. Truth is the light of the sun (cf. Plato); it comes from the Good, which gives it its value (cf. Plato, Republic Book VII).

Truth is the work which results from thought that is pure, not the expression of things themselves.

One begins by considering truth in its relation to things; one ends by considering its value in relation to the mind.

Sacrifice

A. Sacrifice of pleasure.

If one is a reasonable being, there is none because the rule of reason is not a sacrifice, and if one is not a reasonable being and one sacrifices pleasure, it is because one is forced to do so by some other feeling which is more powerful.

B. Self-sacrifice.

[1] Racine, *Phaedra*, ll. 1273–4.

Principle: all belittling of oneself is bad. Sacrifice is related to suicide. It is always something bad to injure one's own power of thought, since thought is the condition of all that is good. Any ability which is not directed towards conscious thought (even philanthropy) must be condemned.

Philosophy and metaphysics

There is no other philosophical enquiry apart from metaphysics.

But one has to see quite clearly that metaphysical enquiry can be thought of in two ways:

It can be looked at from an ontological and from a critical point of view.

Relationships between the scientific, ontological and critical points of view:

Science: has to do with quantitative relationshps between things.

Ontological point of view: one assumes God's point of view. One supposes that one knows things in themselves, and compares them with the knowledge one has of them.

Critical point of view: an attempt is made to become aware of what it is one does in science, etc. The critical point of view tries to compare science as it is with the idea we have of a perfect method. This way of looking at it is quite legitimate, though the ontological point of view is absurd.

Critical philosophers: Plato, Descartes, Kant who introduced the term.

The relativity of knowledge

I   Look for the different meanings of the two words.

II Different domains:

A. Pure sensation: subjectivity.

B. Perception: things appear as being independent of us, but we see everything from a certain point of view or perspective.

C. Science: it tries to do away with perspective. It seems to attain the absolute. But, in fact, it is relative by its relationship to the mind.

III Discussion: this is apparently though not really an argument against knowledge. In fact, the ideal of 'absolute' knowledge would involve submitting to the world. (The Pythian priestess does away with one of the terms of knowledge: the Pythian priestess herself.) It is its relativity that is of value in knowledge, and that even gives the world a value by relating it to the mind.

Error

One can look at it in two ways:

1. Externally: it would then be disagreement with reality.

2. Internally: it then is an incoherence in thoughts. Plato compares those who approach reality with no method at all to blind men walking along a straight road. Likewise, the Stoics speak of the madman who says, in broad daylight, that it is day. Reality has no value in itself since any fool can stumble on it by chance.

So, once we have distinguished between 'true thought' and 'false thought', one ends up by distinguishing 'thinking well' from 'thinking badly'. Error becomes a sin.

Time

Introduction:

Time is the most profound and the most tragic subject which human beings can think about. One might even say: the only thing that is tragic. All the tragedies which we can imagine return in the end to the one and only tragedy: the passage of time. Time is also the origin of all forms of enslavement.

It is the source of the feeling that existence is nothing. Pascal felt this very deeply. It is the way time flies past which makes men so afraid to think. 'Entertainment' is meant to make one forget the course of time. People try to make themselves immortal by leaving things to posterity, but they are nothing but things.

One can bring the introduction to an end by saying that man has an unconquerable urge towards eternity.

There is an insoluble contradiction between human thought, which can never be brought to bear on time (scientific laws), and human life.

Everything beautiful has a mark of eternity. Pure feelings towards human beings: love, friendship, affection (Rodrigue's[1]

[1] Rodrigue – see p. 27, note 1.

feeling towards Chimène, Polyeucte's[1] for Pauline, Dante's[2] for Beatrice). These feelings are not only thought of as eternal, but they consider their object as eternal. So, there is nothing in us which does not protest against the passage of time, and yet everything, in us, is subject to time.

I Subjection to time:

A. The present: what would be left of our thought if we were to leave out of account all the thoughts which have to do with the future and the past? Nothing would be left. So, what we do possess, the present, is something non-existent, which is gone immediately, which is only present to consciousness as something past.

So, by time's law we have no real existence.

This fleeting character of time is the cause of the feeling that one has that life is a dream, that the external world does not exist.

B. Thought: the past is thought of as something which exists somewhere behind one. 'Ou sont les neiges d'autan?' (Where are the snows of yesteryear?) The past has no existence whatsoever. The past is irretrievable, and in so far as it is that, it has an inevitable character about it. The idea one derives from the past is that of inevitability. (Cf. Maine de Biran,[3] 'I have changed.')

The future: appears as chance, and so also as something blind.

So, our helplessness is complete: we can have no influence on the present, because it exists (as soon as the present exists, it is a fact); we can have no influence on the past because it exists no longer; we can have no influence on the future because it is not yet here.

One tries to escape from the feeling of helplessness by entertainment: the excitement of doing something wrong; seeking

---

[1] Polyeucte and Pauline, husband and wife in Corneille's (see p. 27, note 1) play *Polyeucte*. Often thought to be Corneille's finest play, it is set in Armenia and deals with Christian persecution under the Roman Empire.

[2] Dante (1265–1321). Beatrice refers to Beatrice Portmari who is the ideal subject of Dante's love sonnets and lyrics.

[3] Maine de Biran (1766–1824), French philosopher. See his *The Influence of Habit on the Faculty of Thinking*, trans. M. D. Boehm (Baillière & Co., London 1929).

relief in drunkenness (these are base motives; they can be noble: self-renunciation, for example).

II The opposite view:

A. Time is real, the only thing that is real because, even if we think that the world is a dream, it is a dream that is always subject to the passage of time. So, time should be the source of all truths.

Kant: 'Time is *a priori*, and as a result universal.'

One has to overcome a paradox of Bergson: opposition between time and duration (form and matter). Time is something abstract, duration is actual. But he confuses the form and the matter. Time is the only thing that is truly universal. Time is the source of *a priori* knowledge. (What is before cannot be after. Time is irreversible. Between two times there is an infinity of intermediate points, etc.) It is the first thing which gives us the idea of continuity.

B. Time implies eternity.

The relationship between past and future is an eternal one; the very passage of time is eternal.

C. Time, reduced to the abstract form of order, is at the bottom of all eternal truths.

D. The very idea of time implies some kind of grasp on the future: the idea of causality which is of great moral importance.

III Man's weakness and strength. Action which is systematic brings eternity into time.

There are two possible attitudes:

One can either let time roll by (like a little boy with a ball of wool), or one can fill it up; this gives to the passing moments an eternal value.

If one thinks of death as a passing into eternity, one has, of necessity, to think that there was something eternal in life. Cf. Mallarmé[1]: 'So that at last he is changed into himself by eternity.'

---

[1] Stéphane Mallarmé (1842–98), French poet of the symbolist movement. This is the first line of his poem 'Le tombeau D'Edgar Poe'. Mallarmé greatly admired both Poe's prose and poetry, as did Baudelaire, and his poem refers both to Poe and the ideal poet. The first four lines go:

> 'And so at last the eternal changes him
> Into Himself – the Poet with sword unsheathed
> Stirs up his stricken time which knows not how
> In that strange voice the victory was Death's.'

So, the only problem that man has to face, is the struggle against time.

Intuition and deduction

Different senses of the word 'intuition'. Preliminaries.

Intuition is immediate thought.

For Kant: there is 'sensible intuition', but no intellectual intuition. (N.B. 'sensible intuition' is related to sensibility, either by form: space and time, or by content: sensations.)

For Descartes: intuition is the act by which one grasps a relationship.

For Bergson: it is sympathy with the life force.

There is intuition in those cases where one grasps things independently of the intelligence.

In the commonly accepted sense: it is an instinct of divination. What gives unity to these different senses is the notion of an immediate apperception of the mind.

In brief, the subject of this essay is that of opposing 'immediate thought' to 'thought that takes time'.

In conclusion: one has to come to know the value and the limits of these two forms of thought, in what way they go together, etc.

For men, it is an imperfection that they cannot think of everything at once. One thinks of the divine Spirit as being able to think of everything intuitively.

Order to be followed: I. Descartes; II. Kant; III. Bergson and the commonly accepted sense (we move from the senses in which the relation with deduction is most obvious to those where it is the least).

I Descartes.

The limit of intuition is: one can grasp only one relationship at a time. The necessity that belongs to time makes of thought something foreign to itself (to have known is not to know). This kind of thing happens more and more in modern science which has become too complicated.

II Kant's sense of intuition.

The limit is: there is no intellectual intuition.

We cannot get hold of the reality of thinking; proof and verification, these are two separate things.

All intuition is subject to forms of sensibility: man cannot grasp anything that lies outside space and time; all progress in thought is dependent upon sensible intuition *a priori* (arithmetic, geometry) or *a posteriori* (experience). (Analysis of sensible intuition *a priori*: the only way of counting is to count with one's fingers or with objects. Time itself is the matter of this intuition.)

III The commonly accepted sense and that of Bergson.

A. There seem to be different kinds of intuition, not those which make up the steps in deduction as in the previous examples given, but those which take place more quickly and which go further than deduction.

Examples: problems which one discovers all of a sudden; scientific inventions; knowledge of indemonstrable truths (see Pascal[1] on the kind of thought revealed in geometry and that revealed in shrewdness of mind); knowledge of human nature.

B. For Bergson, intuition would be knowledge of the hidden workings of the universe. (Bergson took the commonly accepted sense, and gave it a metaphysical sense.)

Conclusion:

A. Aesthetics: intuitive knowledge is as far as we are concerned an ideal which is never attained. The aesthetic feeling is the feeling that one is going to achieve this ideal, but one never does. That is why there is always suffering in beauty. The beautiful makes us aware of divine thought.

3. Metaphysics: one cannot get hold of things as they are in themselves (there is no intellectual intuition), one can only try to construct their equivalent by deduction. The mind is never in contact with its object. We are subject to irksome constructions, hypotheses, which have to give the best possible account of appearances. Here, as everywhere else, the human condition is such that men move towards something perfect which they never achieve and which they cannot even conceive. Human dignity is to realise this. If one wants to escape from it, one sinks even lower. (Pascal: 'He who wishes to become an angel, becomes a beast.')

[1] See p. 59, note 1.

C. Ethics: the moral law is not something that can be proved; one might say that it is an intellectual insight. The meaning of proofs depends on insight of this kind.

Does introspection enable us to distinguish between voluntary and involuntary actions?

Introduction:

The implications of this question with regard to one's relationship with oneself. Can one have direct knowledge of one's own virtue? Can one think of the will as a power like the passions which is able to overcome them? As existing at the same level as the passions having an existence which can be directly grasped by thought? It looks as if the answer is yes: an act of courage.

I The difference between 'voluntary actions' and 'involuntary actions'.

A. 'Involuntary actions': mechanical reflexes, things done against one's will, clumsy actions.

B. 'Voluntary actions':

1. Intentional actions (for example: taking a walk, applauding in the theatre).

2. Work, it is all the more voluntary when it is work which demands a lot of attention and effort.

3. An act of heroism (resisting torture).

Is there anything in common between the examples under B?

The will in these cases would be the relationship between reasoned thought and what is done, thought determining what is done. What is done exists in a man's mind and is translated into reality.

II A. 1. Mechanical reflexes which appear to be voluntary actions: eating, stretching out one's arms as one falls, walking, closing a window, applauding in a theatre.

In all these cases, the action, which appears to be brought about by judgement, itself brings about the judgement.

In the case of applause in the theatre, one must note the power of social imitation pointed out by Durkheim. In ceremonies men have feelings of delight which they can no longer repeat when they are alone, or which they are unable to recover except by thinking of such moments.

In a religion, one also finds the influence of mass emotions on the individual.

It is very much the same in the case of war, where one finds people who are against war performing heroic deeds.

One could take examples from literature: even Polyeucte, in his enthusiasm as a convert, is under the influence of society.

(Durkheim thought that the difference between actions called voluntary and actions called involuntary was simply that actions called voluntary are those which are the result of reactions which are implanted in the individual by society and actions called involuntary are those which come from the individual alone.[1])

So, the relation between thought and action is reversed. The role of thought as what determines action is an illusion.

2. Are there, nevertheless, cases where thought determines action? In reasoning, one depends on notions which one has not proved; moreover, one is often dependent on chance: in mathematical proofs one often makes construction which one only understands once one has made them. That happens in algebra too. So, even in mathematics, thought follows action.

So we cannot look for the will only in the relationship there is between thought and action.

3. Now, can one by introspection look for the will in action alone? in the gratuitous act? André Gide looked for the will in things which are completely arbitrary (*Caves du Vatican*[2]). But there is no such thing as a gratuitous act: if I say: 'I did it to prove to myself that I am free', there is a purpose involved; otherwise, actions which have no use are reflexes.

C. Finally, can one by introspection look for the will in thought alone?

In deliberation, there is no will since deliberation excludes

[1] Durkheim, *The Division of Labour in Society*, trans. G. Simpson (Collier-Macmillan, London 1964), Bk 2, chapter 5, and *The Elementary Forms of the Religious Life*, trans. J. W. Swain (Collier Books, New York 1961) Bk 3, 'Conclusion'.

[2] Gide, *The Vatican Cellars*, trans. D. Bussy (Cassell & Co., London 1928).

action. Example of Jean Valjean: he was thinking all night but decided nothing, and, in the morning, he acted without a moment's thought.

Conclusion of the second part: the will does not exist, nor, therefore, virtue. We are continually the prisoners of a blind mechanism which even thought can only follow.

III Even this doubt about the value of thoughts is out of gear.

Let us look at doubt and its different kinds:

Mathematics: this means rejecting thoughts to place them in a different order.

In action: reflexes give rise to thoughts. To be free means not to believe them and this changes what we do. (Freedom is itself a way of being.)

Goethe: 'One is aware only of one's faults, one is not conscious of acting correctly.'[1]

(Apply this to the case of skilfulness in sport; to the playing of a musical instrument, etc.)

In this way we come to a wider interpretation of the story about the pharisee in the Gospel.

Conclusion: virtue is the awareness of one's own faults. Humility takes on a different sense from the commonly accepted one; it becomes an intellectual virtue. Virtue goes with self-awareness, but the awareness it implies is awareness of what is faulty, involuntary. The will is what understands, it is not an object of understanding.

Whenever we believe that we understand the will and virtue, it is an illusion. Pride is, above all, an intellectual fault.

---

[1] Goethe, *Wilhelm Meister's Apprenticeship and Travels*, trans. Thomas Carlyle (Chapman & Hall, London 1899), Vol. ii, p. 76: 'No one knows what he is doing while he acts aright; but of what is wrong we are always conscious.' (Niemand weiss was er tut, wenn er recht handelt; aber des Unrechten sind wir uns immer bewusst.) One might compare with what Goethe says in *Poetry and Truth* (trans. M. S. Smith, G. Bell & Sons, London 1913, Vol. ii, pp. 122–3): 'Further, as we generally practise our virtues by a conscious exercise of will, whereas we are unconsciously surprised by our faults, the former seldom procure us any pleasure, while the latter constantly bring with them trouble and pain. Here lies the knotty problem in self-knowledge, one which makes it all but impossible.' The apparent contradiction between these two passages is closely connected with the questions Simone Weil is trying to deal with here.

Attention

Introduction: the importance of the subject.

Attention is what above all distinguishes men from animals.

Is it something which belongs to the mind or the body?

Or, rather, is it dependent on the mind or on the body?

I Spontaneous attention:

Emotion always brings with it attention that is spontaneous (fear, horror, etc.).

Psychological symptoms: one can no longer think about anything else.

Physiological symptoms: motionlessness, tension, holding one's breath.

Is this the only kind of attention?

II Voluntary attention.

One can give an analysis of the attention given to a problem in geometry, or which one gives to an essay one is writing.

Physiological symptoms: quietness.

Psychological symptoms: one doesn't allow oneself to think of anything else, that is to say one suppresses spontaneous attention; for the one excludes the other.

In voluntary attention one is always preventing oneself from becoming tense, and preventing voluntary attention from becoming spontaneous.

III Attention as it is related to the mind and the body.

In any case of attention the part the mind plays in relation to the body is one of control: it does not give it orders, but only stops it from doing certain things.

The mind does not chose the thoughts it wants to have, but shuts out the thoughts it wants to shut out.

Conclusion: the importance of attention:

1. With regard to thought, it avoids errors.

2. With regard to feelings, it prevents infidelity.

3. With regard to action, it prevents sin.

In Paul Valery's *Eupalinos* one can find an analysis of attention in artistic creation.

An artist creates a state of silence for himself and so the soul's forces are marshalled together, but he is not responsible for the inspiration itself; it is in this instant of suspense that he creates; and that instant never lasts long enough. (Compare with the doubt which give rise to Descartes' *Meditations*.)

What makes inspiration possible, is the power to discipline it, to become its master.

Will and the life of the emotions

What part can the will play in feelings, and, in particular, what can it do to bring about or develop feelings of a higher kind?

The will can develop feelings of a higher kind from ones that are lower, but it cannot create them.

What always belongs to it is a power of control.

A. The will can do away with anything that is impure in feeling.

One recognises everything that is impure by the fact that it prevents us from being sincere with ourselves, and by the fact that it is contradictory.

One has to get used to examining oneself, exercising one's own judgement, and finding out how to make one's feelings genuine ones.

Example: in the case of love, and friendship, if the feelings are not pure, one forgets that the object loved has a life of its own.

The relationship between the two beings has to be capable of being reversed; they must be on an equal footing.

So, the purification of feeling is something which belongs almost completely to the realm of thought.

B. On the other hand, what characterises true feeling is faithfulness. Does the will have some influence on faithfulness? One can build up conditioned reflexes: write down the name of the person loved, repeat the things he or she liked saying most, never do what one would not have liked the loved person see us do.

To sum up: feeling of a higher kind can be recognised by two things: truth and faithfulness. Truth belongs to thought, the will to action. The will can never create higher feelings out of nothing: it can always, however, see that they develop out of feelings of a lower kind. So, in fact, it can always create them.

The role of thought in the life of the emotions

Introduction:

If thought does not rule feelings, feelings, certainly, rule thoughts.

Some philosophers (the fideists) think that thoughts are nothing but feelings. But if that is true, we are completely passive.

I Feelings as facts of life. The submission of thoughts to feelings.

   A. Freedom of thought in relation to feelings is an illusion.

Spinoza: 'A child who is annoyed believes it can freely will revenge.'

Leibniz: 'If the weathercock could think, it would say that it turns because it wants to do so.'

   B. Feelings come upon us as the result of chance external events. Spinoza's analysis: the forces of nature are infinitely more powerful than man. So, it is inevitable that man should have feelings.

The fundamental feelings are joy (which is a change to a state of much greater perfection) and sadness (which is a chance to the opposite state).

Whenever something increases or diminishes our body's power of acting, the idea of this same thing increases or diminishes our soul's power of thought. Joy and sadness are elements which are related to the world as a whole. Love is joy accompanied by the idea of an external cause. Hate is sadness accompanied by the idea of an external cause. Anything can be the cause of joy and sadness just by accident.

From the very fact that in contemplating something or other we have experienced joy or sorrow of which it is not the cause, we can love or hate it. We love or hate simply by chance (look for examples in literature).

   C. Our whole life is continuously subject to chance through the influence of feelings.

II One frees oneself from feelings in so far as one understands them.

It is, above all, a matter of understanding that whatever it is, the object exists independently of feeling (love, fear, anger).

For example, for Phaedra, Hyppolytus does not exist.

On the other hand, Augustus, in *Cinna*, understands not only his own attitude towards Cinna, but also what might be the attitude of Cinna and the others to his past crimes.

Turenne shows that he understands his fear when he says: 'You tremble, carcass...'

In antiquity, people were angry with someone who brought bad news (even now that is a natural reaction); it is a matter of understanding that there is no necessary relationship between the news and the messenger, etc.

So, the feeling is still there, but is confined to itself.

III Pure feelings, that is to say ones which are in agreement with rational thought and which are not contradictory.

Instead of quelling one's feelings, one should relate them to something in a way that reason can approve. Then passionate love is changed into platonic love, fear is changed into zeal in face of danger, anger is changed into generosity with regard to its original object and tends to become anger with oneself, horror becomes charity.

All feelings can give rise to love.

The essential character of pure feelings is their unchangingness (which is the essential character of reason).

Conclusion:

Value of feelings in relation to thought. Feelings never allow thought peace, they force it to set about making them pure. Thought makes feeling either something subjective (Descartes) or something objective (Dante).

Imagination in literary creation and in scientific thought

Introduction: commonly held ideas.

A. Imagination constructs all kinds of representations: 'creative imagination'.

B. It begins with the material given to it: 'constructive imagination'.

These two seem to have a part to play in literature and the sciences, apparently in different ways, but when one examines the matter more closely their roles are analogous one to the other.

I Commonly held ideas about creation in literature and in science:

A. Imagination would be the main thing one looks for in literature (the Romantics).

B. A scientist, on the other hand, would be someone who dealt with facts.

C. Still, the scientist can be seen as very closely related to the romantic poet. The scientist too needs a fertile imagination, imagination (speculations about the origin of the world, etc.). Examples: Hertz, Einstein, Cuvier.

II Analysis of the use of imagination in the sciences:

A. Simple examples: problems.

1. Inspired imagination (badly disciplined).

2. Imagination which accompanies step by step a theoretical analysis and cannot do without it.

So, discovering what the problem is means disciplining the imagination.

B. Let us try to understand what systematic invention is.

Example: researches on light (Descartes, Huygens,[1] Fresnel[2]). What one does is to look for the most simple analogy which enables one to reconstruct the observed effects and make it progressively more complex.

Other examples: Hertz, work on electricity.

Conclusion: the imagination is an obstacle one has to bring under control.

III Analysis of imagination in literature:

A. Prose: the writing of a novel does not demand uncontrolled imagination, or, at least, if one forces the imagination one has no success. The novel is a way of controlling an unruly imagination; it controls it by means of thoughts.

B. Poetry: this is a way of controlling the imagination (rhythm, rhyme).

Conclusion: the scientist tames the imagination; the artist creates harmony between soul and body.

---

[1] Christian Huygens (1629–95), Dutch physicist and astronomer, who put forward a wave theory of the nature of light.

[2] Augustin Fresnel (1788–1827), French physicist who studied the diffraction of light and supported the wave theory of light because it provided an explanation of polarisation, whereas Newton's theory did not.

Courage

What are the main forms which courage takes?

Do they have anything in common?

A. One form of courage is to expose oneself to danger, whether this is of active kind (in the case of those who go into battle) or passive (resistance to torture, those who resist fascism).

B. A second kind is that of being cool and collected in the face of danger and suffering (self-control).

C. A third kind is being calm when one is surrounded on all sides by passion.

D. Let us look at the principle that is common to these different forms. One then comes to Plato's definition: 'A true view of what one should and should not fear.'[1]

Conclusion: one should find out how it is related to the rest of the virtue. One ends up with the conclusion not only is there one kind of courage, but that there is only one kind of virtue which consists in self-awareness and self-mastery.

Suicide

I Definition: 'Any action which is done with the idea in mind that it will lead to death.'

II Different kinds:

A. Suicide as a matter of conscience: to refuse to give false testimony under pain of death is in this sense a kind of suicide. To kill oneself if one feels that, if one goes on living, one will become a murderer (German anti-fascists). The ship's captain who sees that others are saved before himself.

B. Suicide for honour's sake: according to the circumstances suicide for honour's sake is more or less like the previous cases. Examples: Cato,[2] Sophonisba,[3] Galois[4] and all those who fight in battles which they do not believe in.

---

[1] See Plato's *Laches*, which discusses the nature of courage.

[2] Cato (95–46 B.C.), M. Porcius Cato, great grandson of Cato the Censor (234–149 B.C.) who used to end all his speeches in the Senate with: 'Carthage must be destroyed.' His great grandson was surnamed Uticensis from Utica, the place of his death, where he committed suicide after defeat in the battle of Thapsus (in N. Africa), because he could not face submitting to Julius Caesar. See Plutarch's description of his death,

C. Suicide through devotion: here one believes in what one is doing; one kills oneself so that others can live: the young Russian terrorists, Decius,[1] Alcestis in Euripides' tragedy.[2]

Acts of suicide for what one is devoted to can be done for the sake of someone else, and this assumes that that person's life is of greater value than one's own, or it can be done on behalf of a number of people: one's country or a church. If so, there is already some despair in it: one denies the value of one's own life for something else.

D. Suicide through despair: in this case, one completely denies the value of one's own life.

Causes: injustice, affliction.

which tells us that Cato after spending the night reading Plato's *Phaedo*, killed himself by stabbing himself below the breast. Caesar when he arrived at Utica said: 'Cato, I grudge you your death, since you have grudged me the glory of sparing your life'.

[3] Sophonisba (235–203 B.C.). See Livy *History of Rome*, Bk XXX, chapters 12–15. Sophonisba, daughter of the Carthaginian general Hasdrubal, and wife of Syphax, the king of Numidia. Syphax was defeated in battle by Massinissa (a Numidian prince who supported the Romans), who, in turn, married Sophonisba to prevent her from falling into their hands. Scipio, the Roman general, was opposed to the marriage and demanded her surrender. In order to spare Sophonisba the humiliation of captivity, Massinissa sent her a bowl of poison with which she ended her life. Sophonisba said when she received it: 'I accept this wedding gift, no unwelcome one, if my husband can do nothing more for his wife. But tell him that I should have died more happily had not my marriage bed stood so near my grave.' Her death is the subject of a number of tragedies by Mairet, Corneille, Voltaire, etc.

[4] Galois – probably a reference to the French mathematician Evariste Galois (1811–32) whose death in a duel could be considered as suicide; though his father, Nicolas-Gabriel, did commit suicide. See E. T. Bell, *Men of Mathematics* (Pelican Books, Harmondsworth 1953), Vol. II, pp. 398–415.

[1] Decius Mus was the name of three Romans who were popularly believed to have secured victory for Rome by 'devoting' themselves and the enemy to the gods below and charging into the enemy ranks to their deaths. The first, Publius, in a war against the Samnites (340 B.C.), his son at Sentinum where, with Fabius Rullianus, he defeated the Samnites, the Etruscans and the Umbrians who had united against Rome, and his grandson at Asculum in the war against Pyrrhus (279 B.C.).

[2] Euripides (480–406 B.C.), Greek writer of tragedy. Alcestis, in his play named after her, the daughter of Pelias and husband of Admetus, sacrificed her own life to save her husband. (See Robert Graves *The Greek Myths*, Vol. I, p. 123.)

III Analysis:

A. One accepts death if one can no longer live without being guilty of, or an accomplice to, a crime, that is an action in which the other person is treated only as a means.

B. One cannot think of the death of Galois as something which might happen to everyone, for example.

C. The point of every one's life is to bring about in the world the greatest amount of humanity possible, One cannot think of something as a duty and think that one will not fulfil it.

Each human being ought to think that he is capable of disseminating thought in the world.

Alcestis delegates this power to Admetus.

Someone who feels within himself that he possesses the means of bringing about the ideal will not die from devotion only if he has as much confidence in another person as in himself. But the moral life is always something which concerns oneself alone. So, even if one feels inferior to someone else, one must feel nevertheless one has some power within oneself.

We should not even ask the question: we should state that we are going to live virtuously.

When it has to do with someone else one always has the right to say: 'I'm not sure about him.' In Euripides, it is quite obvious that the nobler person dies for the coward.

The question is different in the following case: can one accept death in order to save society?

The soldier who dies for his country because he believes that in this way he is making it possible for others to live as human beings, does not commit suicide. But one must have a very clear idea of what one is doing: it must be quite clear that one's death will make it possible for other individuals to think. It is only the conditions of life for mankind as a whole which can take precedence over one human being. By dying, can one prevent human beings from living under a system in which human beings could no longer be human beings?

But one of two things must be the case: if one dies in order to prevent a frightful regime, which nevertheless allows men to live as men, from coming into existence, one has no reason for committing suicide; and if one dies to escape a regime which does not allow men to live as men, one does not die out of devotion, one dies for what is most precious in oneself; for, in any case, one could live no longer.

Conclusion: all forms of suicide, apart from the first, are wrong.

Justice and charity

It is commonly thought that a man who shows charity deserves to be praised, the man who is only just deserves nothing, and the man who acts unjustly deserves to be condemned.

But that is so only because one is thinking of duty from an external point of view: the real demand of justice is to think of each human being as an end (Kant).

The way one states the command of charity: 'Love your neighbour as yourself' is the same as it.

So, in the moral sense, these two statements amount to one. (In the social sense, one is just if one does everything that one has to do in order not to appear before the courts.)

Abstract ideas

A clear distinction must be made between general and universal ideas.

It is possible to have, for example, either a general or a universal idea of a circle. As long as a child does not realise that a circle is produced by the rotation of a straight line about a point, etc. he only has a general idea of what a circle is.

One might say that the advance of knowledge consists in changing general ideas into universal ones.

No idea is general as a matter of course.

Once we have enough biological knowledge to define what a lion is, we shall have a universal idea of what a lion is.

Whenever we bring together things of which we have some notion, but which we are not able to construct, there are only general ideas.

When we reconstruct, we have universal ideas.

We have some notion of what a watch is (a general idea), as long as we have not taken it to pieces and put it together again. (Once we have done that, we have a universal idea of it). Likewise, if one has thought out the principle of the lever in one's mind, one recognises it in all its forms; one has a universal idea of it.

One moves from abstract ideas to things as they actually exist by means of universal ideas.

If, for example, one has the universal idea of the lever, one can study any particular lever by considering the position of the point of leverage etc., one cannot do that if one only has the general idea of a lever.

What is fine about human thought is its ability to move from what is abstract to what actually exists by means of universal ideas.

Bacon: 'Man can only gain control over nature by obeying it'

Introduction:

The general character of human misery and greatness. One has the impression of being sometimes at the centre of the world, and sometimes of being nothing in contrast with it. Man seems sometimes to possess a great power over nature, sometimes to be its plaything.

I Commanding.

Early childhood: an infant rules by its cries; it is an age of magic; desire gains its object through means of speech and gestures. Pagan prayer also has this magical character about it which one finds again in fairy-tales. Even for adults, in these modern times, the world lights up at command, and longed for distant places come to us.

II Enslavement.

Still, death always awaits us, through all sorts of dangers (accidents on a journey, houses which collapse, avalanches, thunder and lightning, etc.); even leaving aside death, one is subject to illness. And, on another level, one is always prey to passions: anger, sorrow, boredom.

So, man is nature's plaything, his apparent power is something that leads him astray; in fact this power does not belong to him; it is given to him and taken away without his knowing why.

III Analysis of the idea of systematic work.

(Spinoza: 'The power through which man continues in existence is limited and is infinitely surpassed by the power of external causes.')

How, with the little power that is his, can man triumph over such fearsome forces? Thought is not a force.

Let us consider actual examples: the domestication of animals – one controls a horse by imposing an obstacle on it (it has to put up with the bit); one controls rivers by dikes; navigation – one uses a rudder to place an obstacle against the water; navigation of sails – when one sails head on to the wind, one is able (by tacking) to use the wind to take one in a direction which is exactly opposite to the one in which the wind would take one if left to itself.

So, one sees that the force of nature is never a controlled force, that nature wills nothing.

It is a matter of conditioned necessity; by changing the cause ever so little, one brings about a great change in the effect. In the case of forces which are completely passive the smallest obstacle has an effect; if one of the circumstances in which force operates is changed, when the force is necessarily changed (not in its own nature, but for the purpose which interests us). The laws which govern natural phenomena are also their conditions; when one is aware of what they are, then one can gain control over nature.

In so far as man believes that there is thought in nature, a force like that which he himself possesses, there are two ways he can look at it; he can either want to control it or submit to it. Whichever he does, he is defeated by it, and is its slave.

It is not by force, but by guile that man can triumph over nature. (This idea comes up again in folk-tales: a giant defeated by a dwarf.)

One can then, describe human action by saying that it is exercised through guile, indirectly that is, according to the conditions of a phenomenon, and not on the phenomenon itself, and that it consists in control.

What is always at stake, as far as man is concerned, is never a matter of concentrating his energy, but of having a method. It is the way the effort is directed, and not the effort as such, which makes human power what it is.

There has to be adaptation.

So where one does not know how to obey, one is powerless. One can command only in so far as one has learned how to obey.

The truth has applications in different fields:

A. The external world: here it is always a question of changing the character of movements (examples already mentioned).

B. Human body: we should learn to serve our bodies, we should not give it orders. For example, one cannot say to one's body: 'Don't be hungry', 'Don't blush', etc. Bacon's statement condemns asceticism. What needs to be done is to use whatever energy is available on other things; passion does not resist something which absorbs our interest. Here, as elsewhere, it is then a matter of transformation of energy.

C. Society.

Example of Napoleon wanting peace,[1] etc.

Conclusion: the recognition of necessity is not only a condition of effective action, but it is also the only thing that makes human life worthwhile.

Plato: 'The Republic'
Book I

Socrates: 'Let us take two men, one who is completely just and yet stripped of everything (even of the reputation of being just) except justice, and another unjust man who is thought of all his life long as a just man. Let us find out who is the happier of the two, assuming that there would be no God to judge them.'

But, since we cannot study justice in the soul, we shall study it in the state.

(The *Republic* is not a political treatise.)

Three classes can be distinguished in the state: 1. the wise; 2. the warriors; 3. the workers.

Plato is looking for the virtue which corresponds to each class:

[1] Perhaps a reference to Napoleon's saying on Elba: 'I want from now on to live like a justice of the peace', when, after his abdication in April 1814, he was granted (by the Treaty of Fontainebleau) the island of Elba as a sovereign domain, an income and a bodyguard.

1. The wisdom of the state is measured by the wisdom of those who direct it.

2. The virtue of the warriors is courage.

3. That of the workers is moderation (needs which have to be controlled).

So, we know what wisdom, courage and temperance in the state will be.

But what will justice be? Socrates defines it as a relationship and harmony between these three orders.

In the soul, Plato finds three principles which correspond to the three classes in the state:

The first, the spirited nature (θυμός), always takes the side of the second, reason, against (the third), desire; it is what makes certain that reason rules desire.

It is only if we treat ourselves violently that we can persuade ourselves to do what has to be done. The spirited nature has to play the same kind of part as a faithful dog does. Justice then is this: it is reason which makes the decisions, it is the spirited element of courage (θυμός) which makes certain that the orders of reason are carried out; it is the desires which obey.

Each principle is legitimate in its own place. If, for example, desire takes a hand in making judgements it is doing the job that belongs to reason, etc.

Once he has found out what justice and injustice are, Socrates goes on to examine the forms of injustice.

Note that Plato defines justice and injustice in a completely internal way. Whatever it is one does, it is just as long as the internal harmony is preserved.

Book VI

Plato thinks that it is only of philosophers that one can say that they see. (But Plato does not deny the external world.)

A philosopher's qualities: he must possess all the virtues. It is to the philosophers that the government of the city must be entrusted. But everyone will say that they are incapable of doing it.

Plato's reply is the simile of the ship.

It is there that one really finds Plato's views about politics.

The owner of the ship stands for the blind mass of people who are the rightful owners of the state; they have to hand over power to someone or other. Here a very important question comes up: is there a science of society?

There isn't one for those who try to seduce the owner (by eloquence), who kill the crew, who drug the pilot, and give themselves up to eating and to amusing themselves. They act violently towards the owner and are quite ignorant of the fact that it would be in their interest to study the stars.

A science of society would do away at once with all those drugged pilots. But those whose lives are ruled by ambition are afraid of the possibility of a science of society, and, besides, the philosophers are few in number, because they have been corrupted by education.

The greatest and perhaps the only danger for the young who have been richly blessed with intelligence is public opinion (sophistry on a social scale). Nowadays the means that exist of making an impression on society on a grand scale are particularly powerful. If one doesn't put questions to oneself and treat things critically, then that is because one has become corrupted by this sophistry which surrounds one on all sides. Something else that stops one is persecution.

The mass of people is a very active, huge beast which reacts quite instinctively and has become completely conditioned; there is a science which enables one to deal with the masses. The fortune of great politicians depends on foreseeing what the great beast will want next. There is a whole philosophy which calls what pleases the great beast 'beautiful', 'good', 'right', and what doesn't please it 'ugly' and 'evil'.

Shall we ever find an individual to tame the great beast? That is what the whole social question amounts to.

In any case, one must at least make a distinction between action and thought, recognise the necessities that are imposed by the great beast, without confusing them with the virtues: justice and truth. The great beast possesses a very powerful collective imagination, but no understanding.

So let us find out what those things are over which the great beast has no power. It has no power over mathematical ideas.

Socrates shows us how philosophers are corrupted. Everyone around them forces them to take power into their own hands. Philosophy is sold. Those who, in spite of everything, are still real philosophers, owe this to particular circumstances: illness. Socrates's demon.

The establishment of a class of guardians: the guardian has to know the perfect ideal.

Nothing imperfect is ever a measure of everything at all.

(This statement can be applied to very many questions, and it states in a nutshell the whole of Descartes.)

It is this idea of the good that gives value of its own to all knowledge.

Knowledge without the idea of the good is just a matter of vanity and curiosity.

The generally accepted idea of what virtue is (which is something quite mechanical) has no real value in it; it belongs to the realm of appearance.

It is possible not to know why one shows courage, moderation, why one is just, etc., all these are but shadows of virtue. True opinion is like a blind man walking along a straight road. Those who have true thoughts without understanding are blind, just as much as those whose thoughts are false. (This has to do with 'chance' both in science and in virtue.)

So let us give our energies to the Search for the Good. What can this Good, which is to the soul what the sun is to visible objects, be? One could call it 'God'. The God of Plato is the God of Descartes: God is beyond known truths: unchanging truths are the result of the relationship between God, the world and ourselves.

Plato and Descartes are two incarnations of the very same being.

Book VII

Allegory of the cave.

The cave is the world.

The fetters are the imagination.

The shadows of ourselves are the passive states which we know by introspection.

The learned in the cave are those who possess empirical forms of knowledge (who know how to make predictions, the doctors who know how to cure people by using empirical methods, those who know what is going on, etc.). Their knowledge is nothing but a shadow.

Education, he says, is, according to the generally accepted view of it, nothing but the forcing of thoughts into the minds of children. For, says Plato, each person has within himself the ability to think. If one does not understand, this is because one is held by the fetters. Whenever the soul is bound by the fetters of suffering, pleasure, etc. it is unable to contemplate through its own intelligence the unchanging patterns of things.

No doubt, there are mathematicians in the cave, but their attention is given to honours, rivalries, competition, etc.

If anyone is not able to understand the unchanging patterns of things, that is not due to a lack of intelligence; it is due to a lack of moral stamina.

In order to direct one's attention to the perfect patterns of things, one has to stop valuing things which are always changing and not eternal.

One can look at the same world, which is before our eyes, either from the point of view of its relation to time, or from that of its relationship to eternity. Education means turning the soul in the direction in which it should look, of delivering the soul from the passions.

Plato's morality is: 'Do not make the worst possible mistake of deceiving yourself.' We know that we are acting correctly when the power of thinking is not hindered by what we are doing. To do only those things which one can think clearly, and not to do those things which force the mind to have unclear thoughts about what one is doing. That is the whole of Plato's morality.

True morality is purely internal.

The man who has left the cave annoys the great beast. (Cf. Stendhal: 'All good reasoning causes offence.')

Intelligence offends by its very nature, thinking annoys the people in the cave.

If one stays in the cave, however easily one will be able to observe all the external rules of virtue, one will never be virtuous. Intellectual life and moral life are one.

What Plato calls the world of what passes away, these are things in so far as one thinks of them in relation to our passions.

One must not say: 'I am incapable of understanding'; one should say: 'I can turn the eyes of the soul in such a way that I will understand.' This equality of minds is a duty, not a matter of fact. (Cf. Descartes.)

The wise have to return to the cave, and act there. One has to reach the stage where power is in the hands of those who refuse it, and not of those whose ambition it is to possess it.

Plato's aim is to find out what forms of knowledge are the right ones to educate those who want to get out of the cave. These are: Arithmetic, Geometry, Astronomy, Music.

Plato's statement about all forms of knowledge:

'They are divine images and reflections of things that are true', so things as they appear to us are appearances of appearances; at least they are this as long as we stay in the cave.

Those who devote themselves to geometry, to the mathematical sciences, grasp what is but as it were in a dream.

So, there is a higher form of knowledge than mathematics which gives an account of the process of thought itself. This is dialectic (νόησις). Unfortunately Plato does not tell us what this higher form of knowledge is. He only states what qualities the dialectician will have: he must be hard-working (physically and mentally), he must hate lying and falsehood.